Ethnologia Europaea

Journal of European Ethnology

Volume 44:1
2014

MUSEUM TUSCULANUM PRESS · UNIVERSITY OF COPENHAGEN

Copyright © 2014 Ethnologia Europaea, Copenhagen
Printed in Sweden by Exakta, Malmö 2014
Cover and layout Pernille Sys Hansen
Cover photo Public domain
Toilet tossing by Crown Prince Willem-Alexander,
Rhenen, April 30, 2012
ISBN 978 87 635 4238 8
ISSN 0425 4597

This journal is published with the support of the Nordic board
for periodicals in the humanities and social sciences.

Museum Tusculanum Press
University of Copenhagen
Birketinget 6
DK-2300 Copenhagen S
Denmark
www.mtp.dk

CONTENTS

MOBOCRACY AND MONARCHY
A Ritualistic Reconciliation with the Anachronism of the Dutch Monarchy

Peter Jan Margry

The relation of the Dutch people towards their monarchy has always been ambiguous. The celebration of the monarch's birthday has become a festive and massive expression of Orangeism, turning the event into a national feast day for all. The celebration is, however, characterized by a certain suspension of rules ("freemarkets") and brings up forms of social inversion und charivaresque behaviour towards the House of Orange. This contribution examines to what extent this seemingly uncritical expression of contemporary Orangeism can be interpreted as a temporary symbolic "mobocracy" that helps to reconcile the nation's republican traditions and strive for modernity with an anachronistic monarchical system.[1]

Keywords: feast, monarchy, rituals, inversion, charivari, social action

During the street fair (*vrijmarkt*) in Amsterdam celebrating the Queen's Birthday[2] and the inauguration of Willem-Alexander as the new Dutch King, on April 30, 2013, a father with his young son set up an orange upholstered throne on the downtown Amstelveld square. Next to it was a sign asking: "What does it feel like to be a king?" For one euro people could sit on the comfortable throne and have a crown placed on their head, while a lackey (the son) provided them with a copy of the *Financial Times*, coffee and refreshments. Being photographed as king for the social media cost 50 cents extra. However insignificant this role reversal might seem, it illustrates the question that I wish to address in this contribution. I will attempt to offer an explanation for an apparent political anachronism: the success-

ful perseverance of the monarchy within modern democratic European nation states. I will do this with the Dutch monarchy as an example.

Orange Mania

In a society that is characterized by modernity and rationalism, the House of Orange (Oranje) continues to enjoy an unusually great degree of support, also in comparison to other European monarchies (Lunshof 2002: 243–246; cf. Schoo 2002).[3] In other words, what makes it possible, or helps make it possible, for the monarchy to be as widely supported in Dutch society as it is? After all, governmental authority often, in one way or another, provokes a certain degree of opposition among people and one of the extreme forms of that authority is a political sys-

Ill. 1: What it is like to be a king: throne, crown and lackey. Amstelveld Square, Amsterdam, April 30, 2013. (Photo: P.J. Margry)

tem with a hereditary monarch as the head of state. As far back as in the 1980s, the sociologist Wilterdink asked why, then, there should be so little opposition to the monarchy in the Netherlands (Wilterdink 1989–1990: 133; cf. Biersma 2002). What is a monarchy doing in a modern bourgeois nation like the Netherlands, where egalitarianism is an implicit credo and being average and normal appears to have become a moral achievement? This kind of reflection has re-emerged in public debate at fairly regular intervals in recent years, often in the context of apparently massive "Orange feeling" and "Orange mania".

This discussion became more insistent in the run-up to the abdication of Queen Beatrix in favour of her son Willem-Alexander in 2013 – an event that moreover coincided with the 200th anniversary of that same monarchy.[4] In this broad discussion in which the Dutch nation asked itself why it exists in the form that is does, it was never the (New) Republican Society that set the terms of the debate, but the discourse was chiefly steered by the "naive" astonishment on this phenomenon expressed by citizens, media and politics itself.

How is it possible that a nation, which invented

itself as a bourgeois republic, should have allowed itself to be saddled with an "artificially" created, authoritarian monarchy in 1813, and down to this very day tolerates it, albeit in a constitutional variant? In my contribution, I will present a new model for explaining the paradox of a "democratic monarchy". A key feature in this discussion is a symbolic temporary "reign" by the Dutch people, a situation that can also be depicted with the term "mobocracy". This term derives from the word "mob" and refers to an irregular rule by groups or masses.[5] For the Dutch case, I give this term a symbolic meaning with respect to the "reign" of the people as well as for its representation of the country's total population.

Although the colour orange is rarely found in nature in the Netherlands, this striking and – in marketing language – "warm-dynamic" tint is emphatically present in Dutch society today. In the Netherlands the colour has a specific political significance as it, traditionally, has been connected with the House of Orange and, since 1813, with the royal house. The historic phenomenon of Orangeism – support in society for the Oranje dynasty – derives from that. However, since the late 1980s the colour orange has had an additional, even more emphatic presence. In that period, the Dutch society massively began to appropriate the royal colour as a form of implicit nationalism for itself (Billig 1995: 93–95).[6] While previously, orange was mostly found in the design of shirts of the Dutch national football team, and in banners, pennants and other decorations around royal and national holidays, these years witnessed an explosion associated with the present Orange mania. The turning point was when the Dutch team brought home the Cup in the European football championship in 1988, and masses of Dutch fans dressed and painted their faces in the national colours, and in particular orange, perhaps combined with a lion costume and a mask, as a reference to the heraldic beast in the royal coat of arms. This "most anarchistic popular celebration ever"[7] was a national event, and marked the beginning of a widely adopted practice which continues to flourish to this day, while peaking at specific celebrative moments, and which is even seen to generate social cohesion (Van der Ploeg 1996; Kullberg 2001, 2004: 18).

The media coined the neologism *oranjegevoel* (Orange sensation, feeling or emotion) for this manifestation. This term began to appear with greater frequency in the media after 1994.[8] Since then, it has frequently been used in the media for both the positive affective attitude in Dutch society towards the royal house, national events or individuals ("heroes") and sports teams, and as a partial explanation for the same phenomenon. *Oranjegevoel* is therefore not a usable analytic term, but much more the description of an emotion. Furthermore, it is an umbrella concept that, because of its suggestive power, is used by the media on any and every occasion. For instance, in late 2012 a major Dutch bank carrying an orange coloured logo started an advertising campaign in which the key word Oranje, capitalized, was paired with a series of important positive values and aims for individuals and the society, in the hope of capitalizing on the positive connotations of Orangeism and Orange sentiments.[9]

The question remains as to just how society itself experiences that Orange feeling. In February 2013, that question was presented through an online questionnaire to a large group of informants of the Meertens Institute in Amsterdam.[10] They were asked to describe what they understood as the "Orange feeling". Roughly, their answers revealed a triple division, which in part connects with what was said above: it was primarily associated with sports and fans ("Orange fever"; with football). A second group associated it rather strictly with the royal house (Orangeism; the Queen's Birthday). And a third group regarded it as a positive flagging metaphor for the Netherlands as a nation, while it was striking how infrequently the word "nationalistic" appeared in their descriptions. On the other hand, the term "solidarity" – a representation of the modern "we-feeling" (cf. Billig 1995: 174) – was frequently associated with it. For the rest, in their answers, this third group often combined the nation with the royal house. As a result, one can say that the second and third categories overlap, while the category of sport remains clearly distinct from these two.[11]

At this point I want to look more deeply at the question of what these latter two forms of the Orange feeling really stand for. I will leave aside the more isolated sports-related expressions, and focus on the phenomenon in relation to the monarchy and the Dutch, in particular when they are combined in the expression of the yearly celebration of the Queen's (King's) Birthday.[12] Should the nationwide expressed Orange mania of that day be regarded as a barometer that refers to a new form of Orangeist loyalty to the royal house, or is the current Orange feeling to be reduced to a nostalgically tinted "folklore" or an expression of a consumerist celebrative culture? Or does the phenomenon perhaps also have social-political functions (cf. Corbin, Gérôme & Tartakowsky 1994)? But before I begin to answer these questions, I wish to briefly indicate how various "traditions" related to the support of the House of Orange – the public presentation of the monarch and the celebration of his or her birthday – have changed over the past century, and how these have contributed to the development of the Queen's Birthday, which was once, symbolically fitting to the content of this article, characterized as "the day par excellence on which the monarch and people shake hands" (Lekkerkerk 1997: 7).

Becoming "Ordinary"

The monarchical political system, which was felt "alien" to the standing ideology of the former Dutch Republic (1588), was created in 1813 more or less by chance, as a consequence of the international political entanglements of that day. At the end of the nineteenth century the Queen's Birthday became a more nationally organized public festive event. The celebration was mainly arranged to celebrate the bonds between the Oranjes and monarchy and the "people". The motive for this can be connected with two central basic political strategies of those days. On the one hand, it was focused on support for the monarchy, to stimulate a national feeling – or "we-feeling" – in everyday life within a society deeply divided by the socio-religious pillarization of the country. On the other hand, the celebrations were a liberal civilizing offensive focused on improving the conduct of popular amusements in general (Van Schoonhoven 2002: 138–140; cf. Helsloot 1995: 299).

The court showed no pronounced ceremonial character, and was then already somewhat reserved and self-effacing (Van Osta 1998: 234–238). Organized as they were by local authorities and Oranje associations, only a limited part of society had the opportunity to express their love and loyalty to the Queen on these occasions, although the royal family were seldom present.

The rapprochement of the monarchy (i.e., the monarchs) in terms of its presentation to and dealings with society began in the twentieth century. It set off an interchange with society in which they adapted to one another in a number of respects, and in some cases took on each other's characteristics. The Queen's (birth-) Day would prove to be a useful stage for the latter, giving the Dutch a new floor and a new position in relation to their royals.

This actually started in the 1950s when Juliana opened the gardens at her Soestdijk palace during the Queen's Birthday celebration in order to decrease the distance to her people. At a respectable distance, from the steps of the palace, the royal family greeted the still carefully selected representatives from society who passed by in review. When after 1952 this observance – the "defilé" – could be broadcast on television, Soestdijk became the epicentre of the Queen's Birthday. The television broadcasts assured that the royal family came into the Dutch homes as individuals of flesh and blood – albeit in mediatized form. Joining these two distant worlds in real-time became an important factor in demythologizing the royal house. During her reign, Juliana made the Dutch adage of "just act normal" her own, as much as possible, perhaps not entirely internalized, but particularly as an outward attitude (Schenk & Van Herk 1980: 69–78). The mass psychologist Jaap van Ginneken noted that the people love the "bicycle monarchy" of the Oranjes because they seem so normal and informal, "they seem like family" (Van Ginneken 2003: 35–36; cf. Jenkins 2002: 4.1–3) – an expression of the Dutch dedication to egalitarianism and rejection of hierarchy.

The long 1960s brought changes to the Netherlands, which did not leave the royal house untouched. Like others of her generation, Beatrix experienced that "the times they are a-changing". Where once the continued existence of the monarchy, legitimized by dynastic continuity, had been defined by myth, distance and distinction, a demythologizing and democratizing of the monarchy to an increasing degree began to take shape.[13] By their new openness and relative simplicity, the Dutch monarchy was able to adapt successfully to the changing ideas and sentiments in society's everyday life.

Increasingly invasive media coverage and a flourishing tabloid press led to the court and royal family becoming increasingly "humanized" and their becoming a public possession. The royal family was included in the network of Dutch celebrities (Brunt 1989–1990: 221–228). According to the Dutch political analyst Jerôme Heldring, the penchant of the younger generation of princes for marrying women from outside the circle of nobility brought with it a dangerous "vulgarization" of the monarchy: "[It is] a consequence of 'wanting to be ordinary', and thus undermines the *raison d'être* of the monarchy, which is not ordinary, and cannot be."[14] It is, however, very much an open question whether this assertion, which reaches back to the views of Walter Bagehot on the British monarchy, also applies to the Dutch situation. To date it would appear that the opposite has proved to be the case, as one can see from the recent "Máxima-effect", coined after the first name of the popular consort of the new King Willem-Alexander.

Another effective strategy for accommodating to the new era was the manner in which Beatrix and her consort, before her ascension to the throne, identified themselves with the avant-garde in intellectual and artistic circles of the time, in a sort of "zeitgeist project". Being involved in activities in a progressive or idealistic context, they created growing sympathy for the monarchy among influential people who would not otherwise have been inclined to support the monarchy. This took the wind out of the critics' sails and what little anti-monarchist sentiment there was, largely remained below the horizon (Wilterdink 1989–1990: 151–152; Huijsen 2013: 328–334). The same strategy would later be employed for Willem-Alexander and Máxima, at the start of the twenty-first century. While there were incidents, the

anti-monarchism was primarily a result of the then general process of democratization and anti-authoritarianism, and expressed itself as a criticism of style and not as a principled rejection of the monarchy (Wilterdink: 1989–1990: 147, 152).

In connection to the previous, arts and culture were expressly instrumentalized for the Dutch monarchy. The arts played an important role as a trait d'union with the society. Beatrix's involvement with modern art, both actively and passively, made her position as the head of state easier (Kempers 1989–1990: 94–95). The wise disposition of cultural capital can divert less desirable attention away from political power or controversial matters. Beatrix also increasingly allowed contemporary artists to depict her or comment on her role in a modern or nonconformist manner in art, or for coins and postage stamps. This too helped create the image of an open, modern monarch, not afraid to step into the domain of irony, divergent views and popularization. Culture has proven to be one of the pillars supporting her reign, expressed in the extensive TV interview with Beatrix in 1988 (Kempers 1989–1990: 94–95).

In a variation on Norbert Elias's power-conditioned "royal mechanism", Wilterdink characterized such a process of adaptation as a "royal strategy": a process in which a royal house opens itself up to society, taking into account various groups in society, whether favourable or critical, with the intention of creating a positive relationship with "potential 'carriers' of anti-monarchism". By applying such a strategy, the House of Orange was able to make the monarchy less controversial than it had ever been before (Wilterdink 1989–1990: 155, 158).

It is said that the apparent paradox of the monarchy is that it is strongly dependent on "form", but that in its modern guise that form and the myth are increasingly disappearing. Thus, the Dutch monarchy is no longer supported by the traditional elite, but has become dependent on the wider population (Schoo 2002: 227, 231). The post-war ascension of Juliana to the throne brought a Queen who from the very beginning in 1948 promoted openness, immediacy and commonality to create such bonding with her people. She already realized that in that era of renewal and reconstruction she had to present her-self to the society in a different way, and that meant as someone who was no different from anyone else in the kingdom, as a person in which her people to some extent could recognize themselves. Her coro-nation speech would prove to be a programmatic statement with regard to this outwardly professed egalitarianism and unpretentious attitude around her, a new phase in which the monarchy and soci-ety grew somewhat closer to one another.[15] It would remove the monarchy further from its stereotypical symbols, court culture and its (moderate) extrava-gance. Her daughter Beatrix would continue in that line. It is now characteristic of the royal family in the Netherlands that they regularly travel by train, or when they travel together on occasions such as the Queen's Day, by motor coach, both means of thrifty communal conveyance that are within the everyday experience of most Dutch people. A new popular fes-tive format for the celebration of the Queen's Birth-day would connect the royal family even more to its subjects and therefore made the popularity of the monarchy within society at large increase.

The Queen's Day – New Style

In the interview mentioned above, from 1988, Beatrix elaborated on her mother's presentation and said of her role as the Queen, "I think you must try to function in such a way that many people can rec-ognize themselves in the totality of the monarchy" (Wouters 1989–1990: 247). That was a mission state-ment about her specific interpretation of her reign. It is not improbable that the "royal riots" during her coronation in 1980, which arose from the squatters' ultimatum "No homes, no coronation" (i.e., housing as a *quid pro quo* for permitting the ceremonies to

Ill. 2: Canals clogged with boats, partygoers and spectators, most of them decorated in orange. Prinsengracht in Amster-dam, April 4, 2014. (Photo: P.J. Margry)

take place undisrupted), and that resulted in a new wave of discontent over the inequalities in society, played a role in the development of her outlook on new forms of royal festive events. Whatever the case, Beatrix had already come to the decision to reinvent the Queen's Birthday observances and no longer celebrate the day with a reception at the palace as her mother did but with encounters on the street. The format and content of the day changed radically (Meijer 1999: 217–226). It is relevant to mention that the actual birthday of Queen Beatrix, January 31, was not celebrated. She preferred to keep the celebration of her own birthday on the birthday of her mother, Queen Juliana, because of the milder weather conditions in spring (April 30), relevant for the mass open-air celebrations and a wide participation.

This new Queen's (King's) Day starts the night before or in the early morning all over Holland. It is like an open market, which is not just a street fair, or an unregulated flea market, as it includes aspects of both and even more than that. It displays – over the whole town, all over Holland – an open stage for musical and theatrical performances and for all kinds of individual playful and comical activities and acts. The day's programme slowly changes from a more family-oriented feast into a massive open-air party event for the younger generations, especially in the cities. None of the parties equals the magnitude of the Amsterdam celebration as it nowadays receives up to 700,000 visitors, who fully clog downtown as well as the canals (with party boats). To keep the partying masses better under control, limitations have been set for the start and the end of the festivities, the sale of alcohol and the amplification of music. In no other European monarchy an equal way of a yearly massive national open-air celebration can be found. Royal birthdays or the monarchy itself ("Constitution Day") are elsewhere usually celebrated in a far more formal way. The popular practice of parodying and mocking the Dutch royal house in a playful way during the proper birthday of the Queen – which will be dealt with in the next section – is equally singular in its kind (cf. Philips 1999; Jenkins 2002: 4.7).[16]

The new Queen's Day celebration format, no longer associated with the royal residence or the observance of the Queen's actual birthday, in a certain sense depersonalized the celebration. This made the monarchy implicitly central to the festivities.[17] In turn, this development has in part been possible due to the years when the Dutch pillarization – the rigid socio-political segmentation of society – was declining; there was a need for a national holiday in the Netherlands, which transcended the divisions in society. Liberation Day (May 5) was for some time regarded as the national holiday that united the country in the post-war era. However, with the war becoming more and more an element of the past and in relation to the country's neo-colonialist status and the new waves of immigration, "liberation" was no longer a suitable heading. At the same time, there was no support for a more "rational" alternative that could perhaps have been more widely appropriated, such as a "Day of the foundation of the nation", an "Independence Day", or a "Day of democracy". Although the monarchy as an institution became more central, that did not appear to be any problem for obtaining broad political support for the new status of the Queen's Day. It has been suggested that the observance is totally separated from politics (Knorr 2012: 121), or as historian Frijhoff formulated it, that it is a strictly communal ritual that has nothing to do with the state (Spiering 1996). However, the festivities have in fact diverse political dimensions. There are two central elements in its significance: first, the celebration is increasingly able to function as *the* national holiday, and second, it is de facto the only opportunity that Dutch society – with its "republican" history – has to periodically and collectively relate to the "alien" institution of monarchy, which the Dutch successfully abandoned already in 1588.[18] How society at large reconciles with the monarchical system nowadays will be discussed below.

Mobocracy in the Netherlands

As said above, one of the socio-political paradoxes in the Netherlands is its acceptance of the monarchy in the context of the contemporary nation state. This is not the case only for the Netherlands; a similar situation exists in several European countries. But

Ill. 3: The kiss, "Give me a kiss, maid": she is one of us and one like us, in *De Telegraaf,* May 2, 1988.

perhaps its existence in the Netherlands is even more remarkable as its monarchy is not purely ceremonial in its functions, and because it is a country that seems to almost have a compulsion to reinvent and renew itself (cf. Kennedy 2010: 43–44). Against this background, it becomes difficult to explain how this society continues to receive unusually high scores in its appreciation of the monarchy, even after the social upheavals of the 1960s and 70s. After all, during those "revolutionary" years there was a possibility to have broken with established, traditional and anachronistic structures (De Rooy 2002: 233–261). While that did happen in various parts of the society, the monarchy remained untouched – something that is also reflected in the statistics. Over the past decades, the regard for the monarchy has hovered between 85 and 87 percent.[19] In 2012, it was still 87 percent; in 2013, the year of Willem-Alexander's accession to the throne and discussions about the monarchy, the figure fell again to 85 percent. Whatever the case, the "national" character of the day lies not only in this high appreciation figure, but also in its balanced observance by neo-colonial and multicultural Netherlands. Even newcomers in the Netherlands find it easy to adapt to this festive ritualistic Orange performance of "citizenship" (cf. Damsholt 2009). As both a national expression of individual experience and as a representative expression of collective feelings, the researcher Paul Kalter saw "our culture functioning optimally" in this celebration (Kalter 1995).

It was only after 1980 that the changes, as a consequence of the previous decades, led to a new public "democratizing" framing for the monarchy. While the coronation riots still could be seen as the last convulsions of the counter culture of that period, an extraordinary event in 1988 suddenly made the extent of the change clear. On April 30, 1988, about a month before the massive outburst of Orange mania as a result of the European championship, Beatrix made a surprise visit to Amsterdam's Jordaan neighbourhood. She was unexpectedly stopped by a resident of the neighbourhood, Maarten Rijkers, who asked her informally to give him a kiss.[20] While she did not do so, she did permit him to kiss her on both cheeks in the traditional continental manner. Photos of the encounter became front-page news, and the kiss took on iconic proportions. Never before had a Dutch monarch permitted herself to be kissed by an unknown subject. The kiss came to symbolize the new relationship with society.[21] The photo reflects the new proximity that Her Majesty "grants" her people, but more than that, it stands for the idea "She is ours, one of us, and really she is just like all of us". Since the days of Juliana this idea of "equality" has been reinforced and perpetuated, and now manifests itself pre-eminently in the Queen's Birthday. An interesting sidelight to this is that this surprise visit to Amsterdam slipped into her schedule because the Government Information Service had begun to fear that there was a growing distance developing again between the royal family and Dutch society. Therefore, they started a PR strategy to improve Queen Beatrix's popularity (Meijer 1999: 218). The monarchy's process of becoming "ordinary" relates to the idea that Jenkins put forward about the requirement of some ordinariness by the Danish monarch to truly represent the nation (Jenkins 2002: 6.4–5). In the Netherlands, the yearly celebration of the Queen's Day ritualizes the royals' seemingly ordinary status.

The phenomenon of social or symbolic inversion can help explain the ways the desire for "equality" on the part of Dutch society was sought after during the Queen's Day. Social inversion is a cultural expression with which a society or group in the society desire to temporarily alter, level out or even reverse existing social relationships and roles in an informal, and often playful manner (Babcock 1978; Manning 1983; Hill 2008). The everyday world as we experience it is then temporarily placed on its head.

In this, the situation affords possibilities to put existing formal structures and individuals (particularly those in authority) in their place, to ridicule them and criticize them. In addition to the general merrymaking that accompanies these occasions, inversion has the function of temporarily obscuring or, on the contrary, of exposing sources of friction in society and easing uneasy relations or structures. Besides that, inversion ritually deals with the issues that arise from the regular relations and hierarchies in daily life. Among the more familiar examples of social inversion are carnival and the church-related Feast of Fools (Van Gennep 1937–1958: 2766–2777; Harris 2011). Carnival is intended to realize an informal equality and familiarity among those celebrating it, temporarily suspending existing norms, giving primacy to ludic language (local dialects) or the vernacular, presenting alternative structures (Prince Carnival, etc.), at the same time providing a safe podium for mockery, and social and political critique (cf. Bakhtin [1941]1984: 196–277; Heers 1983: 240–246; Braun 2002).

In an analogous way, I wish to use this theoretical framework to interpret the meaning of the current celebration of the Queen's Birthday within the context of topicalities as state, monarchy, identity and nationalism in everyday life. In this festive event, the royal family, the local organizers and the individual celebrants and game players form the ritual agents. The royal family is able to mediate equality, populism and democracy, while the other two agents create the full festive experience and the conditions for an open jest season towards the royals, without exceeding the implicit limits of decency. In the whole process, the media are an additional factor necessary to supply information and interpretation and realize interaction among the agents.

As noted above, there is still no satisfactory, coherent explanation for the popularity and success of the new style of the Queen's Birthday, the celebration as it grew into a national holiday and one day unregulated massive festive open market under Queen Beatrix. It is true that many cultural researchers have tried to present an interpretation of the way in which the carnivalesque and chaotic Orange storm is expressed on the Queen's Birthday, but their explanations are often just as banal as the banality that they claim to recognize in the festivities. The sociologist Vuijsje described it as a "revolting drinking spree"; the cultural historian Pleij spoke of "Orange hysteria" and "Orange terror" (Pleij 2003: 77, 94); Meijer, a specialist in the affairs of the Oranjes, characterized it as "coarse sentimentality" (Meijer 1999: 225); and Von der Dunk accused the participants of "infantile tendencies" and "political pathology" (Von der Dunk 2000). Even the Social Cultural Planning Office had no better explanation to offer than to say that it is "a mystery what is really being celebrated". I will try to unravel that mystery.

My point of departure for a new explanation is thus the apparent abnormality of the persisting and even growing strength of the position of the monarchy in a modern, democratic society, and the growth of the Queen's Birthday into the only "real" national holiday that represents both the royal house and the monarchy. In Michael Billig's framing it is the national flagging of shared national identity banally expressed through the present day's Dutch festive culture (cf. 1995: 174–177). The usual explanations for the acceptance of the monarchy during the reigns of the recent monarchs are generally limited to references to a continuing, broad conservative-traditionalist monarchical undercurrent in society on the one hand (cf. Kennedy 2010: 16), and, on the other, the growing pragmatism with regard to the national polity and the modern professionalism, the "Beatrixism", with which Queen Beatrix fulfilled her "profession" (Schoo 2002: 211). In addition, there are references to the phenomenon of festivalizing and the popularity of thematic celebrations (cf. Hauptfleisch 2007). These factors do in fact play an additional role, but to my mind the acceptance of the monarchy at all levels of society is strongly facilitated by the compensatory power of "mobocracy". An inversive "rule" of this nature, in which the population in a certain sense takes the reins in hand and reverse the roles, has its high point during the Queen's Birthday. This "rule" however is of course, by means of the new celebrative format, facilitated by the monarch herself and to a certain extent tolerated by the

authorities. During eve and day, some regulations and ordinances are literally and formally suspended, and the Netherlands is transformed into one great open market in which a good deal is permitted. On the Queen's Day, when the greatest possible collectivity rules public space, the "mobocracy" symbolically carries out its "policy statement". Essentially, the collectivity makes it clear that it is ultimately the boss in a modern democracy. That happens in an apparently uncritical, carnivalesque manner, in the open markets and mass parties that take over the centres of Dutch cities.

Just how massive the celebrations on this occasion are was the subject of an analysis by the Dutch survey agency NIPO. In 2007 and 2008 about 60% of the Dutch population (i.e., about 10 million people, out of 16) celebrated the Queen's Birthday in some way. About half of them (5 million) watched the festivities on television, while 40% (4 million) visited one of the street fairs in 2007. For 2011 NIPO produced other, more specific figures: 33% (5.4 million) of their respondents went to the street fairs, 32% (5.3 million) celebrated it outdoors in their own community, and another 29% (4.8 million) also watched the festivities on television, while 19% did nothing (cf. Knorr 2012: 117).[22] The transformation of the Queen's Birthday from what had been chiefly an event for children into an adult partying event in public collectivity makes it possible to attach political and social-critical notions to the celebration.

Thus, in this political and inversive sense, the Queen's Day also connects with the model proposed by Hauptfleisch, in which the celebration is regarded as a meaningful "eventifying system" (Hauptfleisch 2007: 39–40). That is to say, it is a ludic celebration in which social questions can emerge, not only as innocent or marginal amusement but also through bottom-up social criticism or political commentary pointing to underlying social issues (cf. Manning 1983: 27–30). On the one hand, egalitarianism is expressed symbolically by the widespread appropriation of the family colour orange, while on the other the House of Orange is held up to the light in political commentary and mocking games, while once again referring to their dependent position as servants of the people. It emphasizes that the people, who in their constitutionally guaranteed role as voters could decide on the future of the monarchy, ultimately hold power over them.

For me, the most important characteristic of the Queen's Day is the temporary and reciprocal reversal of social relationships. For example: since the 1980s, the people no longer go to the monarch's palace to pay its respects, but the royal family calls on the people. However, it was Beatrix who out of political reasons personally decided that they would henceforth do so. On that day the royal family symbolically steps down from the throne, as it were, and literally takes a bus to join the people and participate in their everyday affairs. In the two chosen towns or cities that the Oranjes are able to visit that day, the day-to-day dimensions of Dutch traditions and culture in the past and present are acted (or re-enacted) for them. In part, that occurs in traditional activities, but these are organized in a politically correct way, with a multicultural diversity and an artistic and cultural dimension. On the one hand, the royal family are spectators of these cultural expressions of the local community, while being instructed about their significance, but on the other hand they are more or less compelled to participate in the amusements, local customs and cultural activities. Once a year they are then subject to participation in everyday civil life. Reporting on the folkloristic activities during their visit to Sittard, one newspaper used the headlined: "Royal guests dance like ordinary people".[23] In 1996 in Sint Maartensdijk they had to fill sand bags, and a year later in Velsen they were set on a mechanical rodeo bull. Each year they participate in more or less "traditional" Dutch amusements like sack races, pillow fights, the tearing off Dutch cake from a cord with their mouths, run punning mandarin orange races, etc. These are unroyal activities, which they seem to perform dutifully, but which are looked upon with irony by the society or perceived as mockery.

For centuries, jesting, banter and getting people to make themselves look ridiculous have been the pre-eminent means of adding force to inversion. Members of the royal family are by no means immune against this. For many Dutch, the Queen's Birthday is the day-long for writing, drawing or performing something that will mildly make fun of the royal house. The majority of the respondents of the Meertens' questionnaire agreed that the idea of inversion was applicable, and many found the Queen's Birthday to be "*the* moment for poking fun". Others wrote, "it is precisely the moment for jesting, because it is precisely then that we don't need to take the masses seriously", and "poking fun certainly befits a popular celebration".[24] For instance, one considered ridicule necessary "to prevent them from thinking they are too holy or becoming more arrogant than they already are". Short of a complete rejection of ridicule, there were some who laid out qualifications: "with decorum", "nothing gross", "mild jesting, not injurious, cynical or insulting", or "no ridicule, but critique is o.k.". Another characterized it as typically Dutch: "it fits with our national character to take royals like this with a grain of salt." Anything that goes too far and runs into actual *lèse-majesté* will not be accepted by the society, and will result in prosecution. For the rest, *lèse-majesté* is seldom or never encountered on the Queen's Birthday.[25]

The old satirical practice of verbal "shit-slinging" against highly placed persons was seen when a Máxima lookalike sat in a public toilet with the sign "king, emperor, admiral, we all have to take a dump", paraphrasing a riming line in a popular TV ad for toilet paper. In the town of Rhenen in 2012 a new scatological variant was introduced when the Crown Prince was requested to take part in toilet tossing (see cover picture). Before the toss he was given a pair of gloves with darker coloured palms that already suggested faecal stains. Subsequently other competitors of course allowed him to win, and Crown Prince Willem-Alexander took home his prize: a miniature toilet pot. Having a member of the royal house engage in an activity like this fits in the tradition of what in the past was called *charivari*: a public ritual of collective protest against violations of certain norms and values or, in this case, against imbalances in social status (Le Goff & Schmitt 1981: 9). In a *charivari* the positions of the victim and of those performing are defined by their discrepant positions in society. In the case of the toilet tossing the royal family were mocked and put down in a mild way, as the Crown Prince was jestingly put in his place – on the same level as everyone else – via a deeply taboo subject.

A comparable and similarly useful theoretical framework was formulated by the American sociologist Charles Tilly, who investigated how and why ordinary people "make collective claims on public authorities" in times of social and political tension, enlisting repertoires of "popular contention" and "collective action" for this purpose (Tilly 1995: 41–48, 2004: ix). Throughout history, he points to a wide variety of "social movements assert[ing] popular sovereignty" (Tilly 2004: 13, 151–152); imitating and criticizing governmental actions is one of them. In a certain sense, Dutch mobocracy can also be regarded as a social movement, albeit one with an implicit, more symbolic character. It is a movement which temporarily returns power to the people in a more or less playful manner, and which through inversion serves to put the Oranjes on an equal footing with the people. The event is not about a true

Ill. 4: Prince Pils cardboard statue: mocking the Crown Prince's purported studentesque drinking habits. Haarlem, April 30, 2013. (Photo: J. Helsloot)

reclaiming of power by the people, but deals with a reciprocal ritualized subverting of either position. Through the logic of the celebration the involved ritual agents of the Queen's Day also achieve re-establishment and consolidation of the normal order afterwards (cf. Handelman 1998: 63–67).

However that may be, one month after Rhenen it became clear just how close to the edge of legitimacy the toilet ordeal was, when the Crown Prince delicately and indirectly got his revenge on the organizers when he said that he felt ashamed, not for himself, but for the fact that a large proportion of the world's population lack sanitary facilities.[26] With that, he tossed the issue of embarrassment back onto the organizers. For the rest, he was not the only one who was ashamed; many respondents could not get this event, which they felt to be abject, out of their minds either. Although for many this *charivari* went too far, for years members of the royal family have been subjected to similar activities, which were conceived especially for them, and in general done so with little visible reluctance. Some have been things for which people once would have been arrested, for *lèse-majesté*. Beyond these, the monarch herself is usually spared direct confrontational mockery and criticism in the two places that she is visiting. One does, however, find them elsewhere in the open markets. There are always various attractions in which social criticism is focused on the monarch (and her successor). By jeering at them in a playful way, the society as a whole "negotiates" their position and symbolically temporarily takes power. The most popular are various tossing games in which messy objects (eggs, tomatoes, pies, water balloons, wet sponges) are thrown at a target – a picture of the Queen or Crown Prince. Sometimes it is balls that are thrown to knock over Oranje dolls, or one can toss rings over them, or throw darts – or sometimes even shoot a bow and arrow – at royal heads. Dressing up and impersonation is equally common, with drag queen Beatrixes and Prince Pilsmen (referring to Willem-Alexander's purported drinking habits, left over from the years as a student) being far and away the favourites. Old satirical topoi from popular culture resurface when the King is pictured walking a pig or portrayed in a high chair waving his rattle and a piss pot; the background thought is then the ascription of stupidity and immature conduct. One also regularly sees photomontages and posters with texts intended to poke fun at the member of the royal family pictured. The more curious modern variants have included a wood louse race in which each insect bore the name of a member of the royal family, and "maxicosi-curling" in which dolls were thrown into baby buggies to symbolically create offspring for Máxima. As the media always report in detail on the Queen's Day activities, these rituals and jests also reach the royals in a mediatized way. In this way – even when royals were not present – the rituals keep their charivaresque function.

Apart from the ridicule and caricatures that people fire off against the stuck-up, stiff, awkward behaviour and social inequality of the Oranjes, there is one more serious question that keeps returning: money. Although in comparison with other monarchies there is no grand "theatre of the state" to speak of, the finances of the monarchy are perhaps the touchiest issue for the society. Although there is hardly any insight into whether these costs are much higher than if there were a president as the head of state – the general opinion is that they are not – the "royal" aura of even a "modest" monarchy influences the public. This involves not only the structural costs, but particularly the incidental expenses for what is seen as fringe benefits, like a gated exclusive vacation home in poor Mozambique or the upkeep on the royal yacht, "The Green Dragon". In response, on the Queen's Birthday people display photo masks and bare buttocks ("the emperor's new clothes"), or protest banners and direct criticism along the lines of "who's going to pay for this?". But, as long as royal "mistakes" remain in proportion and excuses are made, no noticeable change in the public opinion could be determined so far.

Additionally, for the city of Amsterdam the former City Hall on the Dam – the symbol par excellence of the bourgeois trading nation that made the Netherlands great – remains a sore point. Since Napoleonic times this monumental symbol of the might of the bourgeois republic has been a royal pal-

Ill. 5: Coronation commemorative coin with the masses (the "mob") on the back, 2013. (Photo: public domain)

ace. This "injustice" regularly surfaces in criticism, precisely because the previous and the current symbolism are so in conflict with one another. This has been a recurrent element in the history of the capital city and the Oranjes (cf. Kennedy 2010: 152–157). Some subsequently rename their city with stickers into "Republic Amsterdam".

The abdication and inauguration on April 30, 2013, meant that starting in 2014 there was a transition from a Queen's Birthday to a King's Birthday (April 27). With the accession of the new King, new expressions of mobocratic role-play immediately emerged in society. First of all, asked to do so by the organizing coronation committee, his subjects presented him with a list of their dreams and expectations. The *Droomboek*, containing 6,500 dreams from individual Dutch people, allowed the society to express itself regarding those subjects to which it felt the King should devote his energy.[27] To assist him in that task, an official royal song was created through crowdsourcing, which welcomed Willem-Alexander as the new monarch and at the same time promised him support and guidance from society for his important mission: "We walk with you," sang the participants. The accompanying film clip reaffirmed that visually, with images of a small multicultural cross section of the population, each of whom had raised three fingers on one hand, representing the W of Willem. With that gesture, they swore, as it were, to fulfil their task.[28] From the side of the government, the mobocratic role and position of the people were confirmed numismatically with a special coronation coin, which, apart from the usual portrait of the monarch on the head, also uniquely depicted a "mob", his subjects celebrating the coronation. While it is true that these functions and aims are not expressed in so many words in these projects, they can be interpreted as symbolical illustrations of the new relationship that has been established between the royal house (i.e., the monarchy) and society in the past decades.

Finally, it emerges from the questionnaire that the population nevertheless remain critical, and that the current policy of "tolerance" with regard to the monarchy will depend on the way in which the King fulfils his role. In its considerations the society makes a rational judgement: the respondents' answers frequently suggest, almost with a sigh, that there really does not seem to be any better alternative. When they look at the problems with presidents in surrounding countries, and the costs that go with them, most acknowledge that for them the Dutch monarchy and the way in which it has taken shape, seems to be the least unattractive solution.

Its irrationality is in part redeemed by the Queen's Birthday, the holiday that more than 80% of the respondents see as a form of "bread and circuses", but at the same time is seized upon to take the Oranjes down a notch or two. Only 10% of the respondents of the questionnaire still see the Queen's Birthday as homage to the monarch, which, in the time of Queen Juliana and her *defilé*, was the heart of the celebration.[29]

Conclusion

The question of the governmental "nature" of the Dutch – republican, monarchic or Orangeist – recurs constantly in discussions in Dutch society. Seen from an intellectual-historical perspective, republicanism has some support, but, as many authors[30] have argued, there is no serious disposition to republicanism. The cultural practices related to this issue among the population indicate that the modern nation state can actually get along quite happily with an anachronistic institution like the monarchy. The Queen's Day celebrations are the expression of this, par excellence. Over the past decades that day has developed into the country's national holiday, and is thus no longer a purely Orangeist birthday observance, but a day that celebrates the nation state every bit as much as the constitutional monarchy.

The long 1960s, which saw the crumbling of Dutch pillarization, the arrival of new power relations and growing individualism, called for a modernization of the relation between the society and the monarchy (i.e., the House of Orange). While the starting points for this in the Netherlands, with its modest monarchy, were already favourable, the monarchy itself saw to it that a modernization and the adjustments took place smoothly. Since the Second World War the Dutch royal family started actively positioning themselves as "open", "modern" and "ordinary", as being like their subjects. This strategy precluded too strong objections against the monarchy, and opened up ways for commenting in a more ludic way. Queen Beatrix's idea of redesigning her birthday celebration in 1980 by going "humbly" to her people in the country, elaborated on that. The Queen entering everyday civic life on her own birthday, combined with the of-fer of festive open markets, proved to be a successful formula. The populace could participate in a real national holiday of a truly festive kind and at the same time take on a new attitude with regard to the Oranjes. In connection with a broad repertoire of public ritualistic expressions of derision and *charivari* surrounding the royal family and the monarchy practised during that day, a temporary inversion of relationships and equality has been suggested here. This practice can be seen as a form of "banal" nationalism or Orangeism. The massive celebration of the monarchy on the Queen's Day is not only quantitatively unique among the European monarchies but also in its undisguised mockery and criticism of the monarchy and its royals, made possible by an implicit reciprocal agreement. This is, however, an ironic symbolic construct, which allows the society to – at least provisionally – reconcile its seemingly irrational governmental conduct, and tacitly accept and perpetuate the "anachronism" and the power of the monarchy. The high scores of support of the Dutch monarchy can be explained by this periodic public confirmation of the monarch and the system of hereditary monarchy through the mobocratic behaviour of its people. To this end, the royal house deliberately displays a degree of subservience, while at the same time giving the people what they are entitled to: bread and circuses, while, afterwards, having the royal status reconfirmed. In this, the populace are no objective, single-minded Orangeist movement, but is realized through a multi-layered *imagined community* (Anderson 1983; cf. Billig 1995: 70–73), which continues to support a link between the Netherlands and Oranje for affective, pragmatic or rational reasons. Since this involves a widely accepted idea of a binding force, which is definitive for the existence of the nation, this is also a form of civil religion, which effectively contributes to the continuance of the nation as it is known, and to the well-being of its citizens.[31] And so, on the Queen's Day the whole Dutch society celebrates while celebrating society as a whole nation.

Notes

1 This article was completed on January 20, 2014. Research and writing were done within the context of the project on "Dutchness" at the Meertens Institute in Amsterdam. I would like to express my thanks to the two anonymous reviewers for their comments.

2 Although the feast was called the "Queen's Birthday", the actual birthday of Queen Beatrix was on January 31, but was celebrated on the birthday of her mother: April 30. The birthday of the new King is April 27 (in 2014 however celebrated on April 26) and King's Day will therefore again be celebrated on the proper birthday.

3 Recent approximate average pro-monarchy percentages in national surveys: the Netherlands 86%, Denmark 80%, Norway 73%, Sweden 70%, Spain 49%.

4 See for instance recent media files such as: http://nos.nl/dossier/467420-troonswisseling/; http://www.trouw.nl/tr/nl/13209/Troonswisseling/index.dhtml; www.nrc.nl/troonswisseling/?utm_campaign=footer&utm_source=nrc.nl.

5 This term has been used by Gilje (1987), but differently; he applied the particle "mob" for rioting and violent groups – some hundreds of persons, of all social strata (1987: 289) – against socio-political changes.

6 This apparently recent tradition does need to be placed in historic perspective, in view of the fact that in the nineteenth century – and also before – many people wore orange cockades and bowties. Also after the Second World War it was not unusual to use orange in decorations for the Queen's Birthday, and in scarves etc. worn with other clothing; it is for example recorded that in Oirschot, in Brabant, on April 30, 1949, "everyone had adorned themselves with orange" (Van den Bogaart-Vugts 2000: 105).

7 "26 juni 1988: Het meest anarchistische volksfeest ooit". *Trouw*, May 10, 2008.

8 Based on the newspaper databank Lexis Nexis and the historic newspaper databank at the Dutch Royal Library, it would appear that beginning in 1988 the term was already being used several times a year, initially with particular reference to football, then also to matters related to the monarchy and national affairs. Prior to 1988, the word appeared only ten times.

9 Precisely because the word is consistently used with a capital letter, it may be taken to actually refer to the royal house at the same time. The basic rule in ING strategy was: "Touch the mentality of all The Netherlands: what binds us together and makes us who we are." Thus they appear to suggest that (the colour) orange would touch "the" national mentality and would exercise the same sort of "binding" force as the Oranjes have. For the ING strategy see: http://www.slideshare.net/INGNL/een-nieuwe-communicatie-aanpak-16-nov-2012.

10 The questionnaire was set out via the online "Meertens-Panel" system (see: http://www.meertens.knaw.nl/cms/nl/onderzoek/panel); the 4,761 respondents or informants were asked to answer 11 open questions concerning their views on the "Orange feeling", the Queen's Day, the House of Orange and the monarchy. 1,290 respondents returned a filled-out questionnaire, most citations used in this article all derive from this dataset; not every related citation is therefore separately referred to. The data are stored at the Meertens Institute, a Dutch research institute on culture and linguistics.

11 Questionnaire Orangeism, question 1, 2013, Meertens Institute.

12 Since my research began before the abdication of Queen Beatrix was announced, and is only based on information about the Queen's Birthday festivities, I will continue to use that term here, despite the fact that it has now been transformed into the King's Birthday.

13 Contrary, to a certain extent, to the English monarchy, for example (Billig 1992: 65–85; cf. Gathorne-Hardy 1953).

14 http://vorige.nrc.nl/krant/article1534880.ece (by J.L. Heldring on May 25, 2001), accessed September 10, 2013.

15 In this speech she stated "I want to say emphatically here that for a Queen her task as a mother is just as important as it is for every other Dutch woman", and speaking of her new status, asked "who am I, that I may fulfil these duties?", http://www.histotheek.nl/index.php?option=com_content&task=view&id=376&Itemid=93.

16 Philips (1999) found that the Danish media expressed "mild critique from a position of ironic distance" at a royalist marriage.

17 One point that emerged from a poll done by the *Brabants Dagblad*, April 30, 1997, was that among the alternative terms for the Queen's Birthday, Oranje Day and Day of the Monarchy were regularly mentioned.

18 In 1588, the rebellious Dutch rejected the authority of the Spanish-Habsburgian king and created their autonomous Republic of the Seven United Provinces.

19 The percentages remained more or less stable over these years; with an average of 84% for the monarchy, 9% against, and 7% with no opinion (Wilterdink 1989–1990: 149). In NIPO opinion polls since 1945, even in times of burning royal issues, Biersma found a constant line with percentages of 90% or close to it for and the rest against (2002: 33, 40, 45). Over the last decade the percentage remained stable between 85 and 87 percent; see: http://www.tns-nipo.com/tns-nipo/nieuws/van/steun-monarchie-blijft-stabiel/. For the rest, the methods used in polls of this sort leave little room for nuance, so that it is not clear what they signify and claim to represent (see Glynn et al. 1999 regarding this).

20 It is not clear precisely how the man addressed Beatrix. The family later said it was "Your Majesty" (*Majesteit*); the journalist present heard "Maid" (*Meid*).

21 The kiss is also sometimes regarded as a reconciliation between Amsterdam and Beatrix, on the first occasion when she had appeared among such crowds since the riots at her coronation. A later symbolic reflection of the kiss took place in 2005 when Beatrix greeted rapper Ali B with a streetwise "box".

22 http://www.tns-nipo.com/tns-nipo/nieuws/van/steun-monarchie-blijft-stabiel/.

23 *Brabants Dagblad*, May 1, 1995.

24 Questionnaire Orangeism, question 4, 2013, Meertens Institute.

25 Questionnaire Orangeism, question 4, 2013, Meertens Institute.

26 http://www.ad.nl/ad/nl/1012/Nederland/article/detail/3263323/2012/05/30/Kroonprins-schaamde-zichvoor-wc-pot-gooien.dhtml. Afterwards the Government Information Service was quick to point out that the Crown Prince had participated because the toilets were going to be sent to a development project in Africa.

27 http://www.mijndroomvooronsland.nl/nl-NL/1/hetdroomboek.

28 For the text of the song, see: http://www.youtube.com/watch?v=h_lRn6oBwWY; for the clip: http://www.youtube.com/watch?v=MEUKyKb4g6k.

29 Questionnaire Orangeism, question 3, 2013, Meertens Institute

30 See for instance Huijsen's dissertation: http://dare.uva.nl/document/358682.

31 I have previously defined civil religion as "the religious symbol system which relates the citizen's role and society's place in space, time and history to the conditions of ultimate existence and meaning" (Margry 2011: 6).

References

Anderson, Benedict 1983: *Imagined Communities: Reflections on the Origin and Spread of Nationalism*. London: Verso.

Babcock, Barbara A. (ed.) 1978: *The Reversible World: Symbolic Inversion in Art and Society*. Ithaca: Cornell University Press.

Bakhtin, Mikhail (1941)1984: *Rabelais and his World*. Bloomington: Indiana University Press.

Biersma, Elien 2002: *Oranje ondersteboven? Een onderzoek naar de populariteit van de monarchie*. Thesis University of Amsterdam (FMG).

Billig, Michael 1992: *Talking of the Royal Family*. London: Routledge.

Billig, Michael 1995: *Banal Nationalism*. London: Sage.

van den Bogaart-Vugts, Hanneke 2000: *Hoogtijdagen met en zonder lof: Een onderzoek naar de openbare feestcultuur in Oirschot 1946–1994*. MA thesis Open University.

Braun, Karl 2002: Karnaval? Karnavaleske! Zur volkskundlich-ethnologische Erforschung karnavalesker Ereignisse. *Zeitschrift für Volkskunde* 98:1, 1–15.

Brunt, Lodewijk 1989–1990: Privé: Koningshuis en pers in Nederland. *Sociologisch Tijdschrift* 16:2, 199–229.

Corbin, Alain, Noëlle Gérôme & Danielle Tartakowsky (eds.) 1994: *Les usages politiques des fêtes aux XIXe–XXe siècles*. Paris: Publications de la Sorbonne.

Damsholt, Tine 2009: Ritualizing and Materializing Citizenship. *Journal of Ritual Studies* 23:2, 17–29.

De Rooy, Piet 2002: *Republiek van rivaliteiten: Nederland sinds 1813*. Amsterdam: Mets en Schilt.

Gathorne-Hardy, G.M. 1953: The Democratic Monarchy. *International Affairs* 29:3, 273–276.

van Gennep, Arnold 1937–1958: *Manuel de folklore français contemporain*. Paris: Picard, Maisonneuve et Larose.

Gilje, Paul A. 1987: *The Road to Mobocracy: Popular Disorder in New York City, 1763–1834*. Chapel Hill: University of North Carolina Press.

van Ginneken, Jaap 2003: *Het mysterie Monarchie: Een interview met het Nederlandse volk*. Amsterdam: Boom.

Glynn, Carroll J., Susan Herbst, Garrett J. O'Keefe & Robert Y. Shapiro 1999: *Public Opinion*. Boulder: Westview Press.

Handelman, Don 1998: *Models and Mirrors: Towards an Anthropology of Public Events*. New York: Berghahn.

Harris, Max 2011: *Sacred Folly: A New History of the Feast of Fools*. Ithaca: Cornell University Press.

Hauptfleisch, Temple 2007: Festivals as Eventifying Systems. In: Temple Hauptfleisch, Shulamith Lev-Aladgem, Jacqueline Martin, Willmar Sauter & Henri Schoenmakers (eds.), *Festivalising! Theatrical Events, Politics and Culture*. Amsterdam: Rodopi, pp. 39–47.

Heers, Jacques 1983: *Fêtes des fous et carnavals*. Paris: S.n.

Helsloot, John 1995: *Vermaak tussen beschaving en kerstening: Goes 1867–1896*. Amsterdam: P.J. Meertens Instituut.

Hill, Richard William (ed.) 2008: World upside down = Le monde à l'envers. Banff Alta: Banff Centre Press.

Huijsen, Coos 2012: *Nederland en het verhaal van Oranje*. Amsterdam: Balans.

Jenkins, Richard 2002: Modern Monarchy: A Comparative View from Denmark. *Sociological Research Online* 7:1, http://www.socresonline.org.uk/7/1/jenkins/jenkins.pdf.

Kalter, Paul 1995: Koninginnedag is de parel van onze cultuur. *De Volkskrant*, April 29, 1995.

Kempers, Bram 1989–1990: Vermogend en toch matig: Vijf eeuwen kunst van Oranje. *Sociologisch Tijdschrift* 16:2, 71–107.

Kennedy, James 2010: *Bezielende verbanden: Gedachten over religie, politiek en maatschappij in het moderne Nederland*. Amsterdam: Bert Bakker.

Knorr, Maleen 2012: "Oranje boven": De Nationalfeiertag in den Niederlanden. *Rheinisch-westfälische Zeitschrift für Volkskunde* 57, 117–135.

Kullberg, Jeanet 2001: 'Met voetbal kan het wel, normaal kijk je de buren niet an'. *Amsterdams sociologisch tijdschrift* 28:2, 231–261.

Kullberg, Jeanet 2004: Braziliaanse toestanden. In: *Hollandse taferelen: Nieuwjaarsuitgave 2004 inclusief jaarverslag 2003*. The Hague: Sociaal en Cultureel Planbureau, pp. 13–19.

Le Goff, Jacques & Jean-Claude Schmitt 1981: *Le Charivari: Actes de la table ronde organisée à Paris (25–27 avril 1977)*. Paris: S.n.

Lekkerkerk, Piet 1997: *Koninginnedag met Beatrix: 30 koninklijke bezoeken, 1981–1996*. Woerden: Mingus.

Lunshof, Kees 2002: Republikeinse denkfouten: De monarchie als ware democratie. In: Remco Meijer & H.J. Schoo (eds.), *De monarchie: Staatsrecht, volksgunst en het Huis van Oranje*. Amsterdam: Prometheus, pp. 243–272.

Manning, Frank E. 1983: Cosmos and Chaos: Celebration in het Modern World. In: Frank E. Manning (ed.), *The Celebration of Society: Perspectives on Contemporary Cultural Performance*. Bowling Green: Bowling Green University Popular Press, pp. 3–30.

Margry, Peter Jan 2011: Civil Religion in Europe: Silent Marches, Pilgrim Treks and Processes of Mediatization. *Ethnologia Europaea* 41:2, 5–23.

Meijer, Remco 1999: *Aan het hof: De monarchie onder koningin Beatrix*. Amsterdam: Prometheus.

van Osta, Jaap 1998: *Het theater van de staat: Oranje, Windsor en de moderne monarchie*. Amsterdam: Wereldbibliotheek.

Philips, Louise 1999: Media Discourse and the Danish Monarchy: Reconciling Egalitarianism and Royalism. *Media Culture Society* 21:2, 221–245.

Pleij, Herman 2003: *De herontdekking van Nederland: Over vaderlandse mentaliteiten en rituelen*. Amsterdam: Prometheus.

van der Ploeg, Frederick [Rick] 1996: Koninginnedag-effect: revitalisering van de oude wijken. *Economisch-Statistische Berichten* 81:4046, 155.

Schenk, M.G. & Magdaleen van Herk 1980: *Juliana, vorstin naast de rode loper*. Amsterdam: De Boekerij.

Schoo, H.J. 2002: Hedendaags republicanisme: Een oud politiek idee in de herkansing. In: Remco Meijer & H.J. Schoo, *De monarchie: Staatsrecht, volksgunst en het Huis van Oranje*. Amsterdam: Prometheus, p. 207–241.

van Schoonhoven, Gertjan 2002: "Houd Oranje boven en de troep eronder": De geschiedenis van de nationale feestdag Koninginnedag. In: Remco Meijer & H.J. Schoo, *De monarchie: Staatsrecht, volksgunst en het Huis van Oranje*. Amsterdam: Prometheus, pp. 137–167.

Spiering, Henk 1996: Willem Frijhoff over het "wij-gevoel" van de Nederlanders: een volk van praters. *NRC-Handelsblad*, 3 August.

Te Velde, Henk & Donald Haks (eds.) 2014: *Oranje onder: Populair Orangisme van Willem van Oranje tot nu*. Amsterdam: Bert Bakker.

Tilly, Charles 1995: *Popular Contention in Great Britain 1758–1834*. Cambridge Mass.: Harvard UP.

Tilly, Charles 2004: *Social Movements, 1768–2004*. Boulder: Paradigm.

Von der Dunk, Thomas H. 2000: Oranjegevoel heeft infantiele trekken. *NRC-Handelsblad*, April 22, 2000.

Wilterdink, Nico 1989–1990: "Leve de Republiek": Antimonarchisme in Nederland. *Sociologisch Tijdschrift* 16:2, 133–161.

Wouters, Cas 1989–1990: Informalisering en het Nederlandse vorstenhuis in de 20^e eeuw. *Sociologisch Tijdschrift* 16:2, 230–257.

Peter Jan Margry is Professor of European Ethnology at the University of Amsterdam, and his current research focus is on contemporary religious cultures, cultural memory practices and cultural heritage in the Netherlands and Europe. He is Executive Vice-President of the International Society for Ethnology and Folklore (SIEF). His most recent book (together with Cristina Sánchez-Carretero) is *Grassroots Memorials: The Politics of Memorializing Traumatic Death* (New York: Berghahn Books, 2011).
(peterjan.margry@meertens.knaw.nl)

BETWEEN SOCIAL DUMPING AND SOCIAL PROTECTION
The Challenge of Creating Orderly Working Conditions among Polish Circular Migrants in the Copenhagen Area, Denmark

Niels Jul Nielsen and Marie Sandberg

In a world increasingly challenged by neoliberal restructurings of labour markets within the global economy, labour organisation is continuously challenged. Based on ethnographic fieldwork conducted among Polish construction workers in Denmark, both at their place of work and in their homes in Denmark and Poland, this article traces the objective of creating "orderly working conditions" at insecure and temporary workplaces. The relational analysis – going into work organisation and work/family dynamics – shows how "Polishness" is used as a brand (that the unions need to adjust to) connoting flexibility and availability, and that the composition of the migrant family significantly impacts how migratory practices are made feasible and desirable.

Keywords: East-West migrants, labour mobility, social dumping, migrant families, ethnographic fieldwork

"40 Poles Illegally Crammed Together"
Headlines like this[1] regularly hit the Danish news media. In this case a newspaper article from 2010 reveals that an employer lodged 40 Polish workers in a building approved only for commercial activities, with insufficient sanitary and kitchen facilities as well as serious flaws in safety standards. Such hazardous housing conditions are frequently accompanied with very poor working conditions. The debate that usually arises from such examples point to the deplorable fact that the Danish labour market – once known for its high standards – is deteriorating.

In this paper we explore the challenge of creating "orderly working conditions" at insecure and temporary workplaces that employ Polish migrant wage labourers in Denmark.[2] How these working conditions are negotiated need to be seen in light of the changed influence of labour organisations and the EU free mobility regime. As we will argue, a vital outcome of open borders and weak trade unions is that national self-branding comes to play a central role when wage labourers seek to ensure their wellbeing in changeable labour markets. Migrant workers are no longer simply incorporated into existing labour rights arrangements, a fact which might contribute to making the (Eastern) migrant an intrinsic part of the threat scenario. Media stories, like the one presented above, entail much more than isolated instances of contract violation; they symbolise a situation where an old system of labour organisation is fundamentally shaken.

Through an empirical focus on male circular migrants in the construction industry it will be shown how the difficulty of providing employment with orderly conditions is further complicated by the different ways in which migrants try to establish a feasible and lasting family life.

Labour Movement and Competition – Introducing a New Era?

Not only the Danish but most European labour markets are experiencing profound changes in wage levels and working conditions in the broadest sense. Affected are the realms of security, working hours, permanency of employment, right to holidays, and accruing of pension.[3] Within these developments there is a strong tendency to blame the feared and problematised "Eastern migrants" (cf. Pijpers 2006).

Are these realities part of a new pattern? One could assert that the landscape of enterprises, work sites, and individual labourers searching for work has always been marked by flows, cross-border mobility, and rivalling groups of workers together with varying forms of employer strains, and that these characteristics have been an inseparable part of the supply and demand mechanism intrinsic to the labour market. To some degree, this is true. In the capitalist economy that has run Western societies for more than 150 years, working conditions are constantly changing. In this type of economic system, labourers all essentially compete with each other for available jobs. However, what in the decades following 1900 became the order of the day in most industrialised countries was a labour movement with an increasingly stronger societal footing; this allowed for a reduction in internal rivalry through agreements about working conditions.

Although this development (with considerable variety) took place in most European countries – and despite the self-perception of the labour movement as an association aspiring for worldwide unity of workers – the still stronger position and increasing strength of the movement was first and foremost provided for within the borders of the nation states. National trade unions made agreements with national employer organisations within the limits of acceptability and possibility as viewed by national governments (Jul Nielsen 2004). In that way, the potential competition between workers was kept in check by nationally based systems of organisations, laws and regulations.

This mechanism of the nation state is closely related to the question of migration. For much of the twentieth century, migration was controlled within the frameworks of strong nationally embedded regulation systems. While the years up until WW I were still marked by a somewhat open European labour market, the interwar years – in particular during the crisis of the 1930s – witnessed the closing of national borders, a pattern that continued after WW II. Despite an overall USA-led capitalist economy based on liberal doctrines and the founding of the EEC on similar principles, the European labour markets were not at all marked by free moving labourers and cross-border mobility. As Hansen has keenly illustrated, starting with the boom of the European economy in the late 1950s, which resulted in a severe shortage in labour supply, strong labour unions became highly sceptical of the risk posed by pressure to lower wages in the case of guest-worker migration; and, more importantly, unions had the power to ensure that these workers were granted the same basic conditions as the residential workers (Hansen 2003: 25f.).[4] Also characteristic of this period was the incorporation of guest-workers in the existing labour organisations.[5] Still, the guest-worker migration did not persist; as a consequence of the economic setback in the early 1970s, all countries more or less put an end to the guest-worker schemes. During the following two decades, it was mainly family members of former emigrants and asylum seekers that emigrated, which did not fundamentally shake the labour market system (ibid.).[6]

Neoliberal Restructuring

Crucial for the period in question in this article is, however, the shift that took place after 1990. In the aftermath of the Cold War, a profound liberalisation put its stamp on the European as well as the global economy.[7] Although the EEC had always been based on liberal dogmas, the 1990s introduced a new era. The single European market was formally established in 1993 and a strategy laid out for the EU's "global competitiveness". With these changes, national governments were less able to protect their own companies and their labourers against international competition (Pedersen 2011: 41, 44). One offshoot of this new order was the founding of the World Trade Organisation in 1995 to prevent protectionism and ensure completion of internationally settled liberal agreements. This overall development, usually labelled *neoliberalism*, basically denotes a "fundamental preference for the market over the state as a means to resolve problems and achieve human ends" (Crouch 2011: 7).

In the 1990s, the tenets of the four freedoms – freedom of labour, capital, commodities and services – were given fervent priority; the freedom of labour is obviously of special interest here. An outcome of the Maastricht treaty was European Union citizenship; it gave all EU citizens the right to live, move and work freely in all member countries (Vestergaard & Sørensen 2004: 10). A significant consequence of this new agenda was the loss in influence of labour organisations. Following Crouch's outline of the neoliberal agenda: "… neoliberals are unequivocally hostile to trade unions, which seek to interfere with the smooth operation of the labour market" (Crouch 2011: 18). For most of the twentieth century, unions had the ability to set a societal agenda; today, national workers' associations, if not marginalised, suffer from considerably diminished authority.[8]

It will be interesting to observe how European labour markets respond to the increased liberalisation of post-industrial societies within the global economy; will they increasingly be divided into "A teams" and "B teams"? In this scenario, the B-side is composed of those who do so-called "3D jobs" (Dull, Dirty and Dangerous), that is, the routine, service based and/or risky jobs that secure the safety and health of those on the A-side, who benefit from and to a wide extent also contract such services (Favell 2009: 170).[9] Such dichotomisation of labour markets would certainly increase the demand for a foreign (often also feminised) labour force that is cheap and flexible, "easy to hire and easy to fire" (cf. Pijpers 2010; Sanchez-Carretero 2005). Parallel to the development of the labour market is the probable reorganisation of local communities in host countries where new groups of immigrants attempt to establish settlements (Shutika 2011). In Denmark this is mainly taking place among Muslim immigrants or refugees, while the Polish population is still too small and scattered to put its stamp on whole residential areas. Moreover, the short distance to Poland and the possibility of crossing the border without violating the law means that it is not necessary to make an ultimate decision concerning settlement.

Understanding Open Borders

A supposed consequence of the global economic developments evolving during the 1990s was a "world without borders". This somewhat shabby image has by now been criticised thoroughly (see, e.g., Andersen & Sandberg 2012; Houtum, Kramsch & Zierhofer 2005; Sassen 2008). As is evident from recent developments especially related to migration and the EU's external border regime, Europe's borders are at present undergoing processes of both debordering and rebordering. Furthermore, it is a common misinterpretation that the opening of borders between the European nation states began with the introduction of the EU Schengen agreement. Certainly, the time before WW I can in many respects be regarded as an open border regime where free mobility of the labour force was possible without visas or work permits (Favell 2008, 2009; Kolstrup 2010). Denmark experienced its first wave of Polish labour migrants in the early 1890s and onwards, when seasonal workers were recruited to the Danish dairy farming and sugar industry. This seasonal labour recruitment system was adopted from the German sugar beet farming industry and indeed depended on the possibility of free movement across European borders.

Starting in the 1870s, rural labour from Poland and Galizia entered Germany, a movement known as "going to Sachsen" (*Sachsengängerei*) (Nellemann 1983; Olsson 2007).

In order to grasp the consequences of the open border regime of the present day EU, the emergence of new kinds of territorialities as well as the changeability of the role of the nation state needs to be taken into consideration. Interestingly, this changeability of the state has undergirded its solidity. For some decades now, transnational approaches have pointed out that there is an analytic need for *going beyond* the perspective of the nation state in order to overcome the trap of "methodological nationalism" (Glick Schiller, Basch & Blanc-Szanton 1992; Wimmer & Glick Schiller 2002). The nation state perspective was regarded a trap as long as it remained an unquestioned methodological point of departure as well as an established analytical line of demarcation around a supposedly homogeneous "container" of national culture. Recent contributions, however, and most notably those made by Saskia Sassen, have pointed to the need for *looking inside* the nation state in order to understand how borders are reconfigured and how new forms of territorialities take shape (Mann 2013; Rumford 2008, 2009; Sassen 2009: 587). For example, when foreign companies or agencies establish themselves (or intent to post workers) within another national territory, they do not only refer to national law but also to European law, more specifically the EU Directive for Posted Workers. In effect, new types of bordering as well as novel configurations of the global/national/local occur. Likewise, national employment markets are increasingly Europeanised economically as well as politically. Lubanski (1999) points to the vital role of national tender contracts which according to EU policy should be made as open calls at the European level before the work is contracted. Consequently, any metro or bridge on EU ground cannot be built solely with nationally based contractors unless the tender bid was obtained in equal competition with other European companies. In this respect, transnational changes are potentially developing not only outside and between nation states but also at intra-national venues such as on the pluri-national construction sites and within companies performing work abroad. Importantly, however, the de- and recomposing of the national does not imply that the nation state is erupting or dissolving itself; on the contrary, and as argued by Sassen, processes of "denationalising can coexist with traditional borders and with the ongoing role of the State in new global regimes" (Sassen 2009: 569). In the analysis of the Polish circular migrants, we emphasise how the state is in itself an actor fostering new bordering processes and how various reconfigurations of the actors in the European labour markets play intrinsic parts in these developments.[10]

New Forms of Labour Migratory Practices

The 2004 and 2007 EU accessions opened up novel kinds of border crossings from the new to the old EU member states.[11] The Schengen agreement, providing a political infrastructure that at least ideally eases mobility across borders through the abolishment of working permit requirements as well as passport controls, was broadened to encompass the new Eastern European EU members (Favell, Recchi & Kuhn et al. 2011). This provided the possibility for new types of mobility across the borders of the EU 27, such as shuttle or circular migration, and chain migration.[12] This development fostered yet again national fears of mass migration, in particular anxieties around masses of Eastern European working migrants potentially invading the employment markets and profiting from the social goods of the Western welfare states. In reaction to this, many EU member states including Denmark (and with the UK, Sweden, and Ireland as the notable exceptions) introduced special transitional regulations immediately after the 2004 enlargement. These regulations required working permits from Eastern European working migrants, which can be seen as an attempt to control or at least downscale the expected flows of Eastern working migrants (Kolstrup 2010; Pijpers & Van der Velde 2007).

In the following we shed light on some of the new forms of labour migration we witness after the 2004 and 2007 enlargements and how these practices contribute to a reconfiguration of work places and to new types of migrant/family patterns in Denmark.

Polish Labour Migration to Denmark

In Denmark, Polish workers form the largest group of labour migrants from Central and Eastern Europe, followed by Lithuanians and Romanians.[13] Immediately after the 2004 and 2007 enlargements, most of the Eastern European labour migrants went to the UK, Ireland, Germany, Sweden, presumably due to the absence of transitional regulations in these countries.[14] During the years 2004–2007, approximately 30,000 work permits were issued to Polish workers in Denmark. To this number should be added at least 15,000 posted workers (who are not registered as arrived migrants since they are working for a foreign company) and the unrecorded numbers covering an unknown amount of illegal workers (Kolstrup 2010: 314). According to Statistics Denmark, these numbers are quite stable, with a slight increase in the number of Polish immigrants by a couple of thousand each year since 2005 (Danmarks Statistik 2013).

Most Polish workers take jobs in the building and construction, manufacturing and agricultural industries (Arnholtz & Hansen 2011). However, the (low-skilled) service sector has also seen an increase in Polish work migrants, such as in cleaning services and the hotel and restaurant business. Often these workers are employed through temporary staffing agencies (Kolstrup 2010: 314). As in Norway, the domestic labour force in Denmark has witnessed an increase in Polish migrants (Friberg 2012: 316). The demand for a Polish workforce in Denmark seems to be stable, if not increasing.

Through conversations with central actors in the field (representatives of labour unions, employers as well as contractors) the impression is that the Polish migrants in general have a good reputation among Danish employers and contractors. Mostly, they seem to be known for their flexibility and all-around skills. Interestingly, this picture matches the way the Polish working migrants have managed to brand themselves so as to align perfectly with the ideal of the migrant "flexiworkers" (Pijpers 2010). Although their numbers have not been extraordinarily high, especially when it comes to Denmark, an interesting ambivalence surrounds "the Polish worker", who stands out as an EU intra-migrant, being both a feared and desirable part of the workforce.

Research Design and Ethnographic Material

The following analysis focuses on circular migration within the construction industry. The practices of the migrant construction workers studied can be characterised as circular, as they work in Denmark on a temporary basis, while their families, houses, and in some instances also other jobs are in Poland. Interestingly, the assignment of temporary work contracts abroad is conducted on a more or less regular basis, which means that this type of migratory practice takes the shape of permanent commuting.

Our research has focused on the ways (Polish) labour migration affects the Danish employment market and how various actors are involved in this process. The ethnographic material was collected in 2011–2013 and consists of participant observations from various Copenhagen-based construction sites and in-depth interviews with members of the Polish teams employed at the sites, their Danish colleagues and managers on-site, representatives of Danish labour unions and employer associations, and recruiting agencies and EU politicians. Furthermore, as a part of the relational research design, we have interviewed family members of two of the Polish workers in Poland as well as in Denmark.

Outline of Analysis

Due to the fact that a Polish construction worker can earn a much higher wage in Denmark than in Poland, economic motives are obviously significant. However, simply listing the economic motives of the migrating individuals is not sufficient to address the question of how new kinds of circular migratory practices are made feasible (Sandberg 2012). Concurrently, we follow two approaches to understand the rationales behind circular migrant practices more broadly.

First, we show how the creation of orderly working conditions at the workplace is regarded as an objective for the temporary circular migrants. The migrants in question are eager to do all kinds of jobs and willing to work below their skill sets and professional qualifications. However, this does not imply that the material conditions under which the work is done are insignificant. As we will illustrate, regular payment and clear agreements about working hours are crucial for making mobile livelihoods feasible and desirable, together with less essential but highly valued assets such as the supply of appropriate clothing and access to a heated workman's hut.

Second, we would like to strengthen our analytic understanding of the role of family when exploring the work-lives of the circular migrants. In migratory practices, family members are often left behind. However, just like the migrating family member represents more than one individual's choice to cross borders, in order to access economic benefits, the family members are transformed into a migrant family although they stay in the home country.

We thus investigate how objectives of creating "orderly conditions" are negotiated in practice and how these conditions (fail to) fit with the material-discursive conditions of the migrants' everyday life practices. The second part of the analysis follows the labour migrants in their homes and meetings with their families in order to grasp the various work/family dynamics of the migratory labour practices in question.

Negotiating Orderly Working Conditions

We introduce two different work sites, both located in the Copenhagen area and with the same company owner. The two sites also share the characteristic that Polish teams of workers are employed in projects contracted by the municipality. The first site is a nursing home with facilities for handicapped citizens; the second is communal rental apartments. An important similarity between the two workplaces is that in both cases the Polish teams have a special agreement with the labour union regarding working hours: They work for three or four weeks in a row for 46 hours a week and consequently have the opportunity to visit Poland approximately once a month. In generel, the workers are very pleased with this ar-

rangement. However, although it works well in the context of a commuting practice where the family resides in Poland and time spent in Denmark is dedicated mainly to work, the opposite is the case when the strategy is to build a family life in Denmark.

Included in the agreement is an obligatory, paid membership in the trade union, which is not generally the case among East-West migrants (Larsen 2011). This provides the workers with a wage in accordance with the collective agreement (although not as high as the norm for Danish workers[15]) and access to unemployment benefits. This way of managing working hours is a good example of how a flexible arrangement can be part of establishing orderly working conditions for both employee and employer.

Of further importance are the material working conditions, which seem to be adequate. Working clothes, safety boots and private lockers are emphasised as assets by the Polish workers, as well as a mobile workman's hut to use during breaks. Such orderly working conditions are in stark contrast to previous experiences among the Polish workers in this team, some of whom worked in Berlin during the construction boom of the 1990s as illegal immigrants consequently more vulnerable to exploitation.

The Polish Teams
The two teams consisted of eight respectively nine Polish workers, all male between 25 and 50 years of age. Most of them were married and had children in Poland. Some of the team members were related, and it was apparent that recruitment and jobs were impacted by networks of family and friends.

Within our fieldwork and workplace observations, one 39-year-old man, Karol, played a special role, as we had the opportunity to follow him in various job situations during approximately two years of his employment in Denmark (Jul Nielsen 2013b; Sandberg 2012). Karol is a tile worker, and he has a wife and two children in Northern Poland. In Denmark, Karol earns 19 euro/hour, which is approximately one-third more than he could hope to earn in Poland. In addition, he receives tax allowances due to the fact that he has two households to maintain. According to Danish regulations, tax rates are reduced for people who work abroad, are married, and can prove that they support family in their home country. During our research, we had the chance to witness and visit the different places where Karol has lived: a dormitory sharing one room with a Polish colleague, a small flat where three colleagues were installed, and a rented summer house in South-Zealand. All of these living spaces were spartan, yet functionally equipped. We will later compare the living spaces of Karol's in Denmark with his home in Poland.

The Polish Brand

At the first construction site, several teams are connected to a range of subcontractors and sub-construction firms. Some of the teams are Danish, others are mixed (which is the case among those employed by a staffing agency), one team is Polish, and there is also a group of Serbs working on the site. The Polish team conducts all-around tasks such as providing building materials, preparing the work tasks, keeping the buildings under construction dry, and cleaning up after other workers on the site. When asked, several of the Polish workers revealed that they were well-educated, including for example a technical engineer, tile worker and even a German philologist. It seems, however, to be commonly accepted that professional skills are set aside or at least not put to direct use in the tasks undertaken at the workplace.

As mentioned, the Polish workers are viewed as reliable, punctual and able to do "an honest job" by employers and construction managers. The Danish workers on the site communicated that they were not bothered by having Polish workers do general tasks at the workplace. What we are thus witnessing is the construction of a brand of effective construction workers whose effectiveness is intrinsically connected to their Polishness. This "ethnification" of skills is obviously not connected to genuine differences between Danish and Polish workers. Rather, it is a matter of making a niche for one's work in the labour market. The niche is not linked to professional skills but rather to the fact that the workers come from a low-wage country. In this manner we can observe a Polish self-branding which is crucial to entering and remaining active and attractive in the job market.

At the second construction site the work is organised differently. The teams are more strictly divided; the Polish workers prepare the concrete and make isolations, facades and outdoor structures (terraces of wood). A Danish team from Jutland (the western part of Denmark), where prefabricated elements are produced, commutes to and from the factory to install the built elements and complete all indoor work. Here we see an example of Polish workers doing more professionalised tasks; the niche is different compared to the all-around tasks at the first construction site.

Orderly Working Conditions

A niche can theoretically be spoken of as a monopoly (Jul Nielsen 2002, 2013b): In order to prevent the constant threat of being priced out, a specific group of workers is given exclusive access to specific parts of the work. Such monopolisation always includes some workers and excludes others.[16] If the labour market organisations are involved in the creation of monopolies, both employer organisation and trade union approve the specific arrangement in accordance with the general agreements of the labour market. In this way, open competition between groups of workers is avoided, at least during the contract period.

With the two workplaces we have described two different ways of creating a monopoly, both defining the Polish workers as a clearly demarcated group with access to particular tasks. We have elucidated the rationale – at stake in both cases – seen from the Polish workers' perspective: An orderly arrangement concerning wage and general conditions, including the special working hours agreement, which allows them to sell their work.

What is the employer's perspective in these arrangements? We see this as mainly related to the reductions in the wage budget. Although wages are within the limits of the collective agreement, they are still lower than the overall wage level for Danish workers. As one of the employers states: "We will simply take some Danish instead, if they [the Polish labourers] are on the same level." The Poles are chosen as an outcome of their lower price.

The trade unions enter the arrangement as a necessary sacrifice; it makes it possible to organise – and be attractive to – foreign workers. In other words, a downward pressure on wages is accepted to prevent losing influence with social dumping as a potential outcome. Labour unions can thus maintain the ability to be the recognised negotiator in the labour market.

Therefore, the central question is not simply a matter of whether or not migrant workers adhere to "Danish conditions"; rather, if it is possible for the labour organisations to adjust to the present challenge of including workers from low-wage and low-cost countries without completely losing the ability to set parameters for work conditions.

We now turn to the diverse and contrastive work/family dynamics as another entrance into understanding the rationales of the circular Polish labour migrants from our ethnographic study. First, we introduce three traits crucial for the understanding of transnational families.

Circular Migrant Practices as Work/Family Dynamics

As emphasised by Bryceson and Vuorela, transnational families stand out as an elusive phenomenon to study due to the fact that they are "spatially dispersed and seemingly capable of unending social mutation. Their ability to reconstitute and redefine themselves over time contingent on spatial practicality and emotional and material needs challenges even the most multi-disciplinary social scientist's analytical efforts" (Bryceson & Vuorela 2007: 3).

These researchers made an effort to comprehend the basic characteristics of consanguineously related people, who for some or most of the time live separated from each other across national borders, yet maintain a feeling of unity and "familyhood" (ibid.). It follows that any effort to understand the relationship between labour migrant practices and family life will be challenged by the many different ways they unfold in practice (see also Kofman 2004;

Körber & Merkel 2012; Fog Olwig & Nyberg Sørensen 2001). However, at least three important, basic features are useful to take into consideration when researching migrants' practices related to family.

First, as a number of scholars also stress (Ryan 2009; Bryceson & Vuorela 2007; Grzymała-Kazłowska 2005), "family" must be seen as an entity broader than the household living under one roof, since siblings and grandparents often participate in the arrangements related to migratory practices. Bryceson and Vuorela employ the notion of *family relativisation* to point out "the variety of ways individuals establish, maintain or curtail relational ties with specific family members (…), the modes of materialising the family as an imagined community with shared feelings and mutual obligations" when families are split and living separately (2007: 13). Much of this can be said to apply also to non-transnational families. However, in transnational families the roles and family identities cannot be taken for granted and must be deliberately determined and maintained, since some family members' contributions to the arrangement are paramount.

Second, the age of the involved family members tends to impact the relationship between migrant labour practices and family life. It is thus necessary to include a life course perspective in order to grasp the changing patterns of family relations throughout various life stages (cf. Ryan 2009: 74). The presence of small or young children is probably the most important to consider here due to the manifold obligations children unavoidably imply. Economic migrants commonly reason that the ability to accumulate a satisfying output is to leave their kids behind, at least in the beginning of the migrating process (Zentgraf & Chinchilla 2012: 356). Concerns regarding ageing parents or other relatives can also influence the decision surrounding place of residence (Ryan 2009).

Third, it is important to distinguish between dissimilar basic forms of family/migration patterns. By its very nature, migrant labour – at the lower end of the wage scale – provides an unstable and unpredictable basis for existence. Migrant labour families approach this uncertainty in diverse ways. A main dividing line can be drawn between those that leave the main part of the family back home with only one of the spouses migrating and those that move the whole (nuclear) family. However, it is important to bear in mind that decisions, whether they are of one or the other kind, are not necessarily sustainable. The instability of the employment conditions makes it difficult to make long-term plans. Particularly in the case where the whole family moves in order to settle – at least for a longer period of time – it can prove difficult to cover the increased costs of living that often accompany the higher wage level.

Cross-Border Family/Migration Patterns
As our ethnographic material stems predominantly from the construction industry, the main focus of the following analysis is on Polish transnational families in which the male spouse is working in Denmark. This family/migration pattern – where the husband is the transnational commuter – is of course only one among many, and it is not necessarily a permanent one. It is, however, not atypical, and, more importantly, it is regarded as a basic form by many transnational families themselves, since it aims to combine traditional family values with the conditions of a labour market that encourages migrant work. Our analysis concerns migration within a wage-labour logic where cross-border work must be understood as a means to improve living conditions outside of work. This contrasts with highly skilled migrants, for whom the transnational mobility is rather an element within ongoing career improvement.

In our research, the specific migrant/family life pattern in which the husband is abroad and the rest of the family resides in Poland rested on a mutual agreement between the spouses. This does not necessarily entail a trouble-free arrangement, and it was striking how two aspects of the separation were repeatedly emphasised: its inevitability for improving life perspectives and its temporality. This common understanding appears to be an important condition for holding the geographically separated parts together. Also, it appears that migrant life is understood within a life-course perspective with the eventual objective of stability and old age lived in Poland (or, in some cases, abroad).

Challenges are manifold for a successful family life that is based on cross-border work. The long periods of separation between family members is probably the most important dividing line between transnational families and non-transnational families, and it requires a significant amount of accountability and mutual agreement between the spouses. The migrating partner will be involved in new – and often changeable – settings. Beyond communication, these settings remain more or less unknown to the non-migrating partner: Not only working hours but also spare time and money is spent outside the direct sphere of knowledge or control of the spouse. Vice versa, the migrating partner leaves the child-rearing and everyday family contact to the spouse and, often, to parents-in-law. He risks appearing an unnecessary surplus that the family can manage without. It is in this context that families establish a common perspective regarding the importance of money earned abroad. Not only the spouse but also children and siblings take part in the arrangement, acknowledging the sacrifices that the life of a migrant labourer entails and thus making allowances for the "lacks" accumulated vis-à-vis non-migrant family life. As Zentgraf has pointed out, the acknowledgement and importance made of remittances can be understood in this context (Zentgraf & Chinchilla 2012). Put simply, it is paramount to construe the improvements in the well-being and material status of the family as a direct consequence of the privation of migrant life.

This correlation between cross-border work and family life in Poland can be exemplified through the insights we gained from visiting Karol and his family in the Polish hometown as well as Marcin and his family while they all lived in Denmark. These two migrant families are striking examples of the difference between leaving the spouse and children at home and making a migratory move together in an attempt to establish a life for all family members in the arrival country. Our "entrance" into these insights came through our home visits to the Polish labour migrants, which is why we emphasise the different ways that "home" materialises in the two families' ways of organising themselves (cf. Bendix & Löfgren 2007; Miller 2007). The two families are thus presented as contrasting examples of possible cross-border work/family dynamics.

Two Contrasting Examples
Karol lives with his wife and two sons in an ordinary Polish residential neighbourhood with four-storey buildings. The apartment is filled with the visible outcomes of the husband's migrant work. The two sons have access to modern computers, and several rooms are equipped with flat screen TVs. During our visit the wife prepares a warm lunch for us in the well-equipped and brand new kitchen. The contrast between the humble and scarcely furnished room that Karol inhabits when abroad – often with Polish colleagues – and the home where the rest of the family lives is tremendous. Life in Denmark and life in Poland are like two different worlds, but they are closely knit together and mutually interdependent. To understand one you must know the other. By examining the interior of the apartment, we get an idea of the organisation of this transnational family. It is striking how the commuting father of the family is what we might term *present-though-absent*[17] in every room of the apartment through his tiling of floors and walls, construction of artistically lowered ceilings, and all kinds of do-it-yourself projects. Behind the big sofa lay hidden brand new parquet blocks intended for a replacement of the older living room floor.

As a consequence of the weight put on the positive outcome of working abroad, it is highly problematic if migrant labour fails to produce a surplus. And this is not an unlikely situation in an unstable and precarious labour market, frequently on the margins of regular work relations. The employment situation can change from stable to unstable, leading to periods of unemployment without income, followed by efforts to take on undeclared work. In each case the changed circumstances impact earnings. Extra expenses – maybe paid under the table – for accommodation and travel will often be part of such periods and burden the household budget for the rest of the family. Nevertheless, mutual trust and recognition must be maintained also under such circumstances.

In other words, in order to succeed with a family life that ensures some kind of stability on the terms that migrant labour sets, it seems crucial to create recognition and respect around the family member working abroad to ensure his or her status as an integral part of the family unity despite long periods of separation. In a family where everyone agrees on the arrangement related to cross-border work, the children, depending on their age, often adjust to the special demands by trying not to cause unnecessary concern to their parents. As a whole, the special circumstances will have an impact on them, although it is not possible to generate general statements regarding the consequences of transnational family life upon children (Zentgraf & Chinchilla 2012: 350). What is unavoidable, however, is that children play a significant role in the whole arrangement. In the case of Karol's family, it was striking how the two boys of the family in every respect assisted their parents and the choices they had made through a very supportive attitude. It was evident how the children had been involved in and also adhered to the decisions entailed in the family arrangement.

When the family is residing in the home country it is common for the person staying behind to have some sort of stable, though often low, income. In Karol's family, the wife had a steady part-time job in the municipality, and although this was at the lower end of the wage-scale, it ensured a permanent basic income for the family. This means, however, that the main part of the day is occupied with numerous tasks, since for long periods of time the person staying at home must take over all obligations of running the family: the ever-changing responsibilities surrounding childrearing, food preparation, cleaning and other household tasks, and eventual duties related to other family in the home country. In Karol's family, the son Jacek has participated in cross-border labour assignments during summer breaks. For his 18th birthday, Karol bought a used Ford station wagon for him, which is a clear status symbol both among friends and family members. At 19, Jacek was admitted to his and his parents' ideal course of study at the Technical University in a larger Polish city. Part of the future plan is that Jacek continue working in Denmark during summer breaks, making it possible for him to study full-time the rest of the year in Poland. The father's putting aside of professional skills is thus accompanied by a strong wish of the parents for the younger generation to advance further in educational and social status.

In the type of family life first presented here the home base in Poland is relatively stable and all possible surplus derived from migratory work is used to solidify and expand that base. A stark contrast to this is the example of Marcin, where the whole family endeavours to establish their life in a new country. Marcin is 30 years of age and has been working in Denmark for 6–7 years. He has been working together with Karol in the Polish team for several months. Recently, his wife and (at the time of fieldwork) 11-month-old daughter followed. In the beginning, the wife managed to get a job as a cleaning lady; however, she is now unemployed. The daughter has started at a day care institution, which both parents stress as a significant economic burden. In such a situation it is less likely that the home in Denmark will receive any extra income (when bills are paid and necessary expenses dealt with), since now both parents are subjected to unpredictable working conditions and possible periods of unemployment. Consequently, housing is typically only provisional since flexibility is essential in order for both parts to be able to respond to new job opportunities. This atmosphere of temporariness was reflected in the two-room apartment that the couple had rented in one of the low-price areas at the outskirts of Copenhagen. The apartment is scarcely furnished, and there are relatively few homy markers, such as pictures on the walls, decorations and the like. Extra investments in the home all seem portable. No luxurious or lasting improvements, such as tiling or floor work, were made to the apartment. In contrast to Karol's materialised presence in his decorated apartment despite his migrant work and being abroad for most of the time, this apartment bears witness to the fact that this family has not yet become settled; their apartment is still rather empty. In such a case, the insta-

bility not only applies to shifting work situations but also to family life. There are additional aspects missing here: the elderly generation is not present to assist, and there is a dire lack of knowledge concerning social conditions and rights in Denmark as well as language barriers regarding communication with neighbours, authorities, and welfare officials including care workers. Moreover, expenses are typically higher than those in the homeland. In some cases these complications lead to a strategy where not only core families but extended families – including the older generation and siblings – move together and settle in less attractive neighbourhoods where big apartments are cheap. In the environs of Copenhagen this is the case for instance in Farum and Ishøj. In this way a broader network of support develops, though this does not ensure the flexibility to pursue new work opportunities. Consequently, the family member that earns money might temporarily live apart from the family – only now the division is taking place within the host country.

Migrant working life as a means to improve conditions at home takes the form not only of immediate exchange of earnings for coveted consumer goods but also for long-term dreams and plans. It is a common dream among the Polish construction workers to build or buy a new house when sufficient savings have been made – a house that will be the ideal home for retired life. It is not unusual to see the coveted house appearing as a picture on their mobile phone screen.

The conditions for maintaining close connections to family members in-between[18] have changed significantly during the last decade thanks to information technology. While explaining cultural patterns with technology can lead to technological determinism, it is apparent that the internet and more importantly the broad and relatively easy and cheap access to it have, in basic ways, altered the possibilities for keeping in close and frequent contact with family members (Sandberg 2012). Many of our interviewees are in daily contact with family in Poland through Skype and mobile phones, which, although more expensive to employ, are in regular use. This is in stark contrast to the situation less than twenty years ago when the option for making contact – besides writing letters – was an expensive phone call from a public telephone. For those who prioritise close connections and intimate contact with spouse, children and friends, this has opened up new possibilities and enhanced the chance of being *present-though-absent*.

Concluding Remarks

In the past two decades, increased opportunities to move across borders and gain employment in diversified labour markets has incited opportunities as well as challenges for a growing number of migrant workers. We have highlighted two main concerns surrounding these workers' practices based on our relational study on Polish circular migrants in Denmark: First, we observe an urge to achieve what we term "orderly working conditions". This desire might interfere with the ability to compete for prospective employers who especially value migrant workers if they represent lower costs and higher flexibility. As a consequence, migrant workers are not necessarily likely to generally adhere to the Danish labour market system unless it is able to ensure their competitive advantage over national workers. This is the case in the examples we have presented. Again, we point out the observed difference compared to the previous period of the 1960s, 1970s and 1980s when an ethnic brand such as Polishness did not play such a significant role. Trade unions were much too powerful to allow for that kind of internal competition.

Second, by exploring practices among migrant wage labourers it becomes clear that the labour related migration must be seen as a means rather than a goal in itself. From our study, it seems reasonable to infer that the latter in this case is related to the well-being of the family, whether it moves or stays behind in the country of origin. Thus, despite the large distances and the frequent separations, what takes place in the labour markets and working sites is not only closely connected to but also impacted by the specific organisation of the families that the migrant workers are linked to. Therefore, an important key to understanding behaviours in the labour market is insights into the related family context.

On the political level it is obvious that the higher degree of competition that follows from increased cross-border work migration needs to be counterbalanced by regulations that ensure reasonable social standards avoiding social dumping, whether these are based on union negotiations or legal frameworks. Of relevance here is the relationship between the EU and its member states. We have illustrated the importance of acknowledging state-determined borders, although these probably should be comprehended not only as lines of demarcations but also as domains of authority practiced within and across territories. The way that migrants travel between two or more different regimes of labour market and social regulation is an example of that. Also, it is advisable to focus not only on labour market conditions but also to see migrant lives as different compositions of work *and* family. This concern must also include considerations of a temporal kind regarding whole life spans in order to ensure that working lives based on migrant work – that crosses different legal frameworks of sickness insurance and retirement income – can provide what is necessary also in old age. In sum, conditions must be arranged in a way that makes it possible to attain "orderly conditions" from cradle to grave.

Notes

1 News headline concerning a trial against an owner of an engineering company, *Sjællands Nyheder*, April 27, 2010.

2 The case presented here forms part of a continuing research project on Polish labour migrants in the area of Copenhagen, Denmark, conducted by Associate Professor Niels Jul Nielsen and Associate Professor Marie Sandberg, in the Ethnology Section, the Saxo Institute, University of Copenhagen.

3 With the outbreak of the financial crisis in 2008, this picture is becoming more grim; it is important though, to note that the development was already taking place previous to the crisis. One expression of that was the spreading of the phenomenon of *working poor*, a notion that entails an under poverty-level state of living despite full-time employment (Andreß & Lohmann 2008).

4 Hansen (2003) focuses on West Germany, Great Britain and France in particular, but also claims that similar developments took place in most other Northern European countries including Scandinavia.

5 We can add to Hansen's overall picture a few examples from our research and the research conducted by our students: On the shipyard Burmeister & Wain in Copenhagen the first wave of "foreign workers" in 1969 was without question assimilated into the union system (Jul Nielsen 2013a). At a big steel works in Northern Zealand it is reported that in 1970 incoming foreign labourers from Yugoslavia were immediately led by a union representative to the union office for their assignment as they approached the train station (student interview, 2011, made by Kristine Gårdhus and Galit Peleg).

6 That is as a consequence of migration. In Great Britain the labour organisations were severely challenged by the politics of the conservative government. The 1980s were generally a weak period for the labour side, but in other countries changes were less notable. In Denmark the government support of the employer side in relation to a huge strike wave during 1985 was a sign of a more generally changed agenda (Jul Nielsen 2004: 321f.).

7 See, among many others, Crouch (2011).

8 Here is not the place for a discussion of what lies behind this development – a changed production pattern and the end of the Cold War are probably the two most prominent reasons (Jul Nielsen 2004) – but it embraces the challenge of migration with a principally new framework compared to the 1960s, 1970s and 1980s.

9 The term "3D jobs" was originally used to characterise the cross-border labour migration system evolving at the US-Mexican border. This is where we see a clear example of the development of parallel labour markets with a more or less permanent demand of cheap services provided by usually illegal workers (Düvell 2009; Favell 2009).

10 For a further elaboration of what might constitute a state as "an actor" of a principally other kind that might be key to understand the persistent presence of mutually related "state subjects", see Bolving & Højrup (2007) and (www.lifemodes.ku.dk). For a discussion – based on an analysis of the development throughout the twentieth century – of the theoretical relation between the role of state sovereignty and the basic conditions of wage labourers, see Nielsen (2004).

11 Cf. similarities with former historical periods pre-WW I, see the section above.

12 Whereas circular migration and shuttle migration refer to migratory patterns that are based on migrant practices working temporary abroad (although this could be on a permanent basis), the concept of chain migration depicts the new inflows of labour migrants entering the East and Central European countries, such as Ukrainian labour migrants in Poland (Kindler 2012).

13 According to The National Labour Market Authority the numbers of foreign workforce with a registered income in Denmark were in 2013: 1) from Poland: 24,189, 2) from Rumania: 9,326, 3) from Lithuania: 9,078. Source: *Arbejdsmarkedsstyrelsens database Jobindsats. dk. Udenlandske statsborgere med lønindkomst i Danmark.*

14 Further has Norway, as according to Friberg, become one of the top migrant destinations among Poles with around 140,000 Polish migrants arriving between 2004–2011 (2012: 316).

15 This tendency of Eastern migrants to be placed at the lower steps of the wage ladder is part of a general pattern, cf. Andersen & Felbo-Kolding (2013).

16 A monopoly will always be temporary. The particular borderlines between different work areas will over time be exposed to changes according to fluctuations of power balances between wage earners and employers. During major transformations, like the one we are undergoing in these years, this is particularly the case; that is why we witness how dividing lines between trades, skills and functions are submitted to grave alterations.

17 Here the notions of absence and presence are applied in order to depict the gap between the observed closeness of the relations within the family and real life conditions for being together. The absence-presence figure could also be seen through Derrida's notion of *différance*, which relates to the poststructuralist idea that whatever the form of an object (or phenomenon, expression or ritual), this also implies a set of absences. Along this line of thought absences are not *non*-existing but temporarily postponed, which makes an object a pattern of presences and absences. Inspired by STS-scholar John Law (2002, 2004), the absence-presence figure is further discussed and applied in Sandberg (2009a, 2009b).

18 Importantly, this applies not only to spouse and children but, dependent on their importance in the family/migration pattern, also to other relatives (Ryan 2009: 63f.; Vuorela & Bryceson 2007: 3; Körber & Merkel 2012).

References

Andersen, D. & M. Sandberg 2012: Introduction. In: D. Andersen, M. Klatt & M. Sandberg (eds.), *The Border Multiple: The Practicing of Borders between Public Policy and Everyday Life in a Re-Scaling Europe.* Aldershot: Ashgate Publishing Limited.

Andersen, S.K. & J. Felbo-Kolding 2013: *Danske virksomheders brug af østeuropæisk arbejdskraft.* Copenhagen: FAOS.

Andreß, H.J. & H. Lohmann 2008: *The Working Poor in Europe: Employment, Poverty and Globalisation.* Northhampton: Edward Elgar Ltd.

Arnholtz, J. & N.W. Hansen 2011: Nye arbejdsmigranter på det danske arbejdsmarked In: T.P. Larsen (ed.), *Insidere og outsidere – den danske models rækkevidde*. Copenhagen: Jurist og Økonomforbundets Forlag.

Bendix, R. & O. Löfgren 2007: Double Homes, Double Lives? *Ethnologia Europaea* 37:1–2, 7–15. Copenhagen: Museum Tusculanum Press.

Bolving K. & T. Højrup (eds.) 2007: *Velfærdssamfund – velfærdsstaters forsvarsform?* Copenhagen: Museum Tusculanum Press.

Crouch, C. 2011: *The Strange Non-Death of Neoliberalism*. Cambridge, UK; Malden, MA: Polity Press.

Danmarks Statistik 2013: *Indvandrere i Danmark*. November 2013, Copenhagen.

Düvell, F. 2009: Migration, Minorities and Marginality: New Directions in Europe Migration Research. In: C. Rumford (ed.), *The SAGE Handbook of European Studies*. Los Angeles, CA; London: Sage, pp. 329–346.

Favell, A. 2008: The New Face of East–West Migration in Europe. *Journal of Ethnic and Migration Studies* 34:5, 701–716.

Favell, A. 2009: Immigration, Migration, and Free Movement in the Making of Europe. In: Katzenstein (ed.), *European Identity*. Cambridge etc.: Cambridge University Press, pp. 167–189.

Favell, A., E. Recchi, T. Kuhn, J. Jensen & J. Klein 2011: *The Europeanisation of Everyday Life: Cross-Border Practices and Transnational Identifications among EU and Third-Country Citizens*. State of the Art Report, EUCROSS Working Paper no. 1. Chieti: Universitá di Chieti-Pescara.

Fog Olwig, K. & N. Nyberg Sørensen 2001: *Work and Migration: Life and Livelihoods in a Globalizing World*. London; New York: Routledge Research in Transnationalism.

Friberg, J.H. 2012: The "Guest-Worker Syndrome" Revisited? *Nordic Journal of Migration Research* 2:4, 316–324.

Glick Schiller, N., L. Basch & C. Blanc-Szanton 1992: Transnationalism: A New Analytical Framework for Understanding Migration. In: N. Glick Schiller, L. Basch & C. Blanc-Szanton (eds.), *Towards a Transnational Perspective on Migration, Race, Class, Ethnicity, and Nationalism Reconsidered*. New York, NY: New York Academy of Sciences Annals of the New York Academy of Sciences, pp. 1–24.

Grzymała-Kazłowska, A. 2005: From Ethnic Cooperation to In-Group Competition: Undocumented Polish Workers in Brussels. *Journal of Ethnic and Migration Studies Journal of Ethnic and Migration Studies* 31:4, 675–697.

Hansen, R. 2003: Migration to Europe since 1945: Its History and its Lessons. In: S. Spencer (ed.), *The Politics of Migration: Managing Opportunity, Conflict and Change*. Malden, Mass.; Oxford, UK: Blackwell, pp. 25–38.

Houtum, H. van, O. Kramsch & W. Zierhofer 2005: *Bordering Space*. Aldershot: Ashgate.

Jul Nielsen, N. 2002: *Virksomhed og arbejderliv, bånd, brud-flader og bevidsthed på B&W 1850–1920*. Copenhagen: Museum Tusculanum.

Jul Nielsen, N. 2004: *Mellem storpolitik og værkstedsgulv, den danske arbejder – før, under og efter Den kolde krig*. Copenhagen: Museum Tusculanum.

Jul Nielsen, N. 2013a: Arbejderen mellem praksis og ideologisering 1850–2000. *Kulturstudier* 1, 58–81.

Jul Nielsen, N. 2013b: Grænseløse arbejdere – en diskussion af identitet og selvbevidsthed med udgangspunkt i polske migrantarbejdere. *Arbejderhistorie: Tidsskrift for historie, kultur og politik*, pp. 44–60.

Kindler, M. 2012: *A Risky Business? Ukrainian Migrant Women in Warsaw's Domestic Work Sector*. Amsterdam: Amsterdam University Press.

Kofman, E. 2004: Family Related Migration: A Critical Review of European Studies. *Journal of Ethnic and Migration Studies* 30:2, 243–262.

Kolstrup, S. 2010: *Polske stemmer: Polske indvandringsbølger 1892–2008*. Copenhagen: Frydenlund.

Körber, K. & I. Merkel 2012: Imagined Families in Mobile Worlds. *Ethnologia Europaea* 42:2, 5–11.

Larsen, T.P. 2011: Den danske model og dens insidere og outsidere. In: T.P. Larsen (ed.), *Insidere og outsidere – den danske models rækkevidde*. Copenhagen: Jurist og Økonomforbundets Forlag.

Law, J. 2002: On Hidden Heterogeneities: Complexities, Formalism, and Aircraft Design. In: J. Law & A. Mol (eds.), *Complexities: Social Studies of Knowledge Practices*. Durham: Duke University Press.

Law, J. 2004: *After Method: Mess in Social Science Research*. London; New York: Routledge.

Lubanski, N. 1999: *Europæisering af arbejdsmarkedet: Bygge- og anlægssektoren i Tyskland, Danmark og Sverige*. Copenhagen: Jurist- og Økonomforbundets Forlag.

Mann, M. 2013: *The Sources of Social Power*. Volume 4. New York: Cambridge University Press.

Miller, D. 2007: "Why the best furniture goes to the house you can't live in". *Ethnologia Europaea* 37:1–2, 45–49.

Nellemann, G. 1983: *Polske landarbejdere i Danmark og deres efterkommere: Et studie af landarbejderindvandringen 1893–1929 og indvandringens integration i det danske samfund i to generationer*. Copenhagen: Nationalmuseets forlag.

Olsson, L. 2007: Polish Migration to Denmark and Sweden before World War I. *Przeglad Polonijny* XXXIII:4, 63–72.

Pedersen, Ove Kaj 2011: *Konkurrencestaten*. Copenhagen: Hans Reitzel.

Pijpers, R. 2006: "Help! The Poles are Coming": Narrating a Contemporary Moral Panic. *Geografiska Annaler* 88B:1, 91–103.

Pijpers, R. 2010: International Employment Agencies and Migrant Flexiwork in an Enlarged European Union. *Journal of Ethnic and Migration Studies* 36:7, 1079–1097.

Pijpers, R. & M. Van der Velde 2007: Mobility across Borders: Contextualizing Local Strategies to Circumvent Visa and

Work Permit Requirements. *International Journal of Urban and Regional Research* 31:4, 819–835.

Rumford, C. 2008: *Citizens and Borderwork in Contemporary Europe.* London: Routledge.

Rumford, C. 2009: *The SAGE Handbook of European Studies.* Los Angeles, CA; London: Sage.

Ryan, L. 2009: Family Strategies and Transnational Migration: Recent Polish Migrants in London. *Journal of Ethnic and Migration Studies* 35:1, 61–77.

Sanchez-Carretero, C. 2005: Santos y Misterios as Channels of Communication in the Diaspora: Afro-Dominican Religious Practices Abroad. *Journal of American Folklore* 118:469, 308–326.

Sandberg, M. 2009a: *Grænsens nærvær og fravær: europæiseringsprocesser i en tvillingeby på den polsk-tyske grænse.* Copenhagen: Det Humanistiske Fakultet, Københavns Universitet.

Sandberg, M. 2009b: Performing the Border: Cartographic Enactments of the German-Polish Border among German and Polish High-School Pupils. *Anthropological Journal of European Cultures* 18:1, 87–93.

Sandberg, M. 2012: Karol's Kingdom. *Ethnologia Europaea* 42:2, 87–93.

Sassen, S. 2008: *Territory, Authority, Rights: From Medieval to Global Assemblages.* Princeton; Ewing: Princeton University Press.

Sassen, S. 2009: Bordering Capabilities versus Borders. Implications for National Borders. *Michigan Journal of International Law* 30:3, 567–597.

Shutika, D.L. 2011: *Beyond the Borderlands: Migration and Belonging in the United States and Mexico.* Los Angeles: University of California Press.

Vestergaard, A.M., C. Sørensen & Dansk Institut for Internationale Studier 2004: *Østudvidelsen og arbejdskraften: Myter og realiteter.* Copenhagen: Dansk Institut for Internationale Studier, DIIS.

Vuorela, U. & D. Bryceson (eds.) 2007: The Transnational Family: New European Frontiers and Global Networks. In: D. Bryceson & U. Vuorela (eds.), *The Transnational Family: New European Frontiers and Global Networks.* Oxford: Asociación de Antropólogos Iberoamericanos en Red (AIBR).

Wimmer, A. & N. Glick Schiller 2002: Methodological Nationalism and beyond: Nation-State Building, Migration and the Social Sciences. *Global Networks* 2:4, 301–334.

Zentgraf, K.M. & N.S. Chinchilla 2012: Transnational Family Separation: A Framework for Analysis. *Journal of Ethnic and Migration Studies* 38:2, 345–366.

Niels Jul Nielsen, Ph.D., is Associate Professor of Ethnology at the Saxo Institute, University of Copenhagen. He has for a number of years investigated industrial culture related to labourers and work. The research is currently undertaken within the collaborative project Neoculturation of Life-Modes during the Current Transformation of State System and World economy (lifemodes.ku.dk).
(nnielsen@hum.ku.dk)

Marie Sandberg, Ph.D., is Associate Professor of Ethnology at the Saxo Institute, University of Copenhagen and member of the steering group of Centre for Advanced Migration Studies (AMIS), University of Copenhagen. Research themes are borders and their current transformations within Europe and beyond, together with European East-West migration and new forms of mobility across borders.
(sandberg@hum.ku.dk)

QUANTIFIED CYCLISTS AND STRATIFIED MOTIVES
Explorations into Age-Group Road Cycling as Cultural Performance

Stefan Groth

Building on ethnographic work with German recreational cyclists, this paper analyzes competitive motives in hobby races and training. Laying open the construction of non-competitive recreational sports as part of the dichotomy between work and leisure, the analysis turns to competitive stimuli in performative experience and examines their effects. These range from short-term efforts in races and group rides to the structuring of training and race schedules. Looking at how motives fluctuate between different layers of competitiveness, three main developments and currents influencing road cycling are observed: the popularity and possibility of big urban events, the increase of quantification, the transparency and availability of data and knowledge, and the permeability of life worlds to competitive norms.

Keywords: mass sports, road cycling, rationalization, quantification, competitiveness

When Jan Ullrich secured the victory of the 84th Tour de France in July 1997, after placing second behind Team Telekom teammate Bjarne Riis one year earlier, professional road cycling became massively popular in Germany. "Il Kaiser," as Ullrich was nicknamed by Italian newspaper *Gazzetta dello Sport*, attracted the attention of German viewers for a sport that had been on the lower levels of the national sports hierarchy for a long time. Viewing figures of public broadcasters skyrocketed to up to 3.38 million viewers per stage, images of Ullrich in the leader's "maillot jaune" (yellow jersey) occupied the covers of major newspapers, sales figures for road bikes increased considerably and social democratic parliamentary party leader Rudolf Scharping accompanied the Grand Tour stage race clad in Team Telekom kit.

Enter 2013: Ullrich and many of his former teammates admitted to doping, only 12 of the 26 podium finishers since 1997 have not been penalized for taking forbidden substances, the main television broadcasters have dropped professional road cycling from their programs entirely, and newspapers only rarely fail to mention past doping scandals in reports on a discipline with one of the strictest anti-doping policies in professional sports. Scharping – now president of the influential *Bund Deutscher Radfahrer* (BDR, German Cycling Federation), the national governing body of cycle racing in Germany – pleads for the re-introduction of Tour de France television coverage against a myriad of critics and corruption charges against cycling's world governing body, the Union Cycliste Internationale (UCI, International Cycling Union). Notwithstanding, road cycling itself has gained in popularity over the last couple of years.

There is a peculiar disconnection between road cycling as a mass and recreational sport, on the one hand, and competitive cycling, on the other hand. Contrary to the dictum of the "role model function" of competitive sports for their leisure time pendants (Gieseler & Palm 1985: 5; Wann 2001), recent developments suggest the thriving of cycling as a mass and recreational sport despite the fall from grace of the discipline's professional elite, and not because of its popularity in the public eye (see Feddersen, Jacobsen & Maenning 2009 for a study on this "growth paradox" in tennis). Even though the "new generation" of young German professional cyclists – outspoken against doping and demanding severe sanctions against dopers – is highly successful in international races, the sport's stigma remains clearly visible. Similarly, the decline of the amateur portion of road racing – that is the competitive branch of the sport where licensed riders compete in local and regional races, but are, unlike professionals, not paid for it – has been diagnosed by many due to unattractive and unspectacular races with few spectators. More and more riders choose not to "draw a license" in the three available performance categories, and the BDR fears the demise of their system of competitive road racing. However, the sport itself is highly popular: Hobby races in road cycling have especially seen an immense increase over the last couple of years, and while the number of professional races in Germany has decreased, the number of participants and the level of professionalization of age-group races show a steady rise. As many as over 20,000 hobby riders take part in so-called "Jedermann" (everyman) races, and sponsored teams with substantial budgets, training camps and former professional and amateur riders are becoming more frequent. Road cycling on the level of mass and recreational sports in Germany, it seems, is in transition.

This transition is characteristic not only for road racing, but for many other disciplines in mass and recreational sports as well. Urban marathon and triathlon events with sumptuous supporting programs have been – despite costly participation fees – attracting thousands of international participants, and arouse the interest of city marketing, the hospitality industry and sponsors alike. The estimate for the self-proclaimed "sports city" Frankfurt's "City Triathlon" with 1,700 finishers is that the average participant spends 500 euros during the stay in the city (FAZ 2012a), creating significant economic incentives for planners and the sports industry. Similar developments have been observed for road cycling over the last couple of years, and they come as somewhat of a surprise and challenge to the organizational system as well as to available frames of interpretation available for road cycling as a mass and recreational sport. This article will take this element of surprise as a starting point to investigate these developments that have not been thought to be possible and shed light on some aspects that have enabled the current processes. Building on work from the sociology of sports (Cachay & Thiel 2000; Winkler & Weis 1995) and ethnological approaches to sports (Bausinger 2006; Besnier & Brownell 2012; Husmann & Krüger 2002; Palmer 2002), I am interested in the configurations where sports as an integral part of everyday culture are subject to profound shifts in meaning and manifestation, calling into question long-standing understandings of why and how actors engage in sportive activities in mass and recreational sports. These shifts, I will argue, are related to a changing understanding of the body in the social sciences (Gugutzer 2006) and the rhetorical construction of social subsystems – from sports and work (Rigauer 1969) to sports and non-sports – as interdependent, but separate domains with corresponding distinct frames of interpretation. Furthermore, drawing from recent developments in an anthropology of competitiveness (Tauschek 2012, 2013), I will analyze the embeddedness, relativity and stratification of competitive motives in hobby races and training, along with a focus on technological developments enabling the creation of new frames for interpreting and evaluating performance and performance progressions. My goal in this paper is to lay open the immediacy of competitive stimuli in performative experience and its effect both in its ephemeral and persistent dimensions, stretching from short-term efforts in races and group rides, to the structuring of training and races schedules, and lastly to the appropriation of discursive registers and underlying semiotic processes mediating motives between different layers of competitiveness. I will suggest that there are three main developments and currents influencing the situation in road cycling: the popularity and possibility of big urban events, the increase of transparency and availability of data and knowledge, and the permeability of life worlds to competitive norms and economic principles (cf. Götz 2013). My data are drawn from research conducted at hobby races and group rides in 2012 and 2013, including participation in races and interviews with cyclists and organizers. I will begin by discussing the history and current situation of road racing in Germany against the backdrop of the development of sports in modern society. I will then deal in greater detail with the Jedermann scene in Germany and its particularities, before looking at specific cases as illustrations of broader qualities of modern recreational sports and their entanglement with society and cultural values. These cases are presented as a means of exploring multifaceted analytic perspectives on the field of road cycling as an example of sports in modern society.

Sports, Society, Culture, and Cycling

Ranging from functionalist approaches analyzing the role of sports in different historical contexts (Plessner [1956]1997), to the perspective of systems theory viewing sports as a subsystem interdependent on and relating to other social subsystems (Bette 1999), and to Frankfurt school theorists criticizing sports as an extension of the fetishization of instrumental reason (Morgan 1988; Rigauer 1969), the pervasive force of sportive activity, both as spectator or participant activity (Bausinger 1990), is widely acknowledged. The import of sports in everyday culture has led to declarations that sports are indeed culture, with specific, yet permeable, norms of practice and understanding (Hitzler 1991), and contribute to the formation of individual and collective behavior, perception and interpretations. Sports and society influence each other mutually, and consequently, sports have become a significant "cultural pattern" among others (Bausinger 2006).

The genesis of sports as a sociocultural phenomenon is closely linked to the emergence and development of civil society. According to Elias' and Dunning's figurational sociology, the history of sports can only be adequately understood by viewing it in the context of the process of civilization. Focusing on the interrelation between sports and "society at large," they argue that playing by the rules in sports is a way to practice social standards:

> [S]ports involve a playing with norms on two levels: with those norms which are specific to the sport itself and with those characteristic of the society at large, with those of "non-leisure" life. … Sport, moreover, provides a good example of the variety of ways in which people can find ways and means for de-routinisation, for the "de-crustation" of self-control and of the emotional restraint imposed upon them in societies such as ours. (Elias & Dunning 1984: 150)

This "emotional refreshment" and relaxation of affect control provided by the physical activity of sports was, according to Elias and Dunning, one of the needs of industrialized societies. In the development of sports in England in the mid-nineteenth century, it was hoped that regulated competitive games such as cricket, partly replacing more brutal sports such as rugby or recreational pursuits like hunting in school curricula, could fulfill an integrative function (Hartmann-Tews 1996: 53f.). Not surprisingly then, there were moves towards an authoritative notion of sports favoring some kinds of sport over others, resulting both in the demotion of folk games (Johler 2003) and popular (*volkstümliche*) soccer games (Elias & Dunning 1984: 85). The idea that certain kinds of sport and competition can have a positive effect on the socialization and integration of citizens prevailed in England and many other parts of the world (Digel 2012: 71). In that perspective, sport is a means for a controlled and limited expression of excitement and suspense in a regulated society, in the beginning catering mostly to a select group of aristocrats and upper class citizens.

Similarly, cycling started as a bourgeois and male privilege. After the rise of early race events in the late-nineteenth century, the competitive aspect was discouraged and the focus was shifted to a "gentlemen's pastime" (Cox 2008: 2) by official cycling associations in the UK (Woodland 2005) and Germany (Gronen & Lemke 1987). Cycling became more and more a domain of the working classes with the availability of cheaper bike models. Again, races were initially frowned upon and professional racers were barred from the main organizations; only slowly did the model of professional and paid athletes replace the "gentleman amateur" racing for splendor rather than income. France was the forerunner in this development that led to "the myth of the racing cyclists as working class heroes" (Cox 2008: 4; see also, Dauncey 2003). In Germany, post-WW I depression amplified this process as unemployed men participated in track and road races under harsh conditions in hopes of earning a living. In Nazi Germany, amateur and professional cycling and other competitive sports were largely disestablished in favor of physical exercise for all (Bernett 1966) aimed at maintaining the health of the "racial corpus" and to combat laziness, lameness and indifference (Schäfer 2011a, 2011b).[1] However, the successes of track racers, such as Gustav Kilian and Heinz Vopel, taking part in six-day races in the United States, were still used for propaganda purposes.[2]

After WW II and up until the early-1960s, club sports in Germany were predominantly embedded in the semantics of competitive activities for young men (Cachay & Thiel 2000: 116), mainly constricted to performance-oriented motives; only slowly did the structure of sports organization change to favor a more inclusive paradigm of "sports for all" (Hartmann-Tews 1996). This development had an influence on cycling as a mass sport as well. Noncompetitive biking excursions had always been popular in

Germany, and the early-1970s saw the introduction of road bikes and cycling kit (special jerseys and shorts) in organized cycling tours as a popular and successful format by the BDR.

Despite only a tangential interest in professional races and riders, cycling as a mass and recreational sport was growing. The latter two were thought to be influenced less by competitive norms and more oriented towards fitness, enjoyment and conviviality. Both in scholarly discourse and in the view of the sport's main organizations, mass sports were commonly defined as all sportive activities under the umbrella of organized sports clubs (Cachay & Thiel 2000: 116), and not carried out in a competitive manner (though team sports evade this definition). Beginning in the early-1980s, numerous mass sports campaigns were initiated, targeting all age groups and classes and stressing the positive benefit of sports for all for society (cf. Kurz & Storck 1994). Recreational sports, on the other hand, were seen as more openly and individually organized and not confined to club structures, but comparably free from competitive motives (Dieckert 2002). As leisure activities, both definitions situate sports outside of work life, and construct – despite acknowledging the interrelations and mutual dependencies of sports and society at large – conceptually different spheres with divergent logics of practice and interpretation. No doubt, the clear cut dichotomy of leisure as passion and work as necessity is still upheld and widespread.

However, these definitions and distinctions became heavily contested from the 1970s onwards, initiated – among others – by Bero Rigauer's *Sport und Arbeit* (translated as Sports and Work, 1969). Rigauer argued that the distinction between the worlds of sport as a mode of leisure, on the one hand, and work, on the other hand, was invalid, because the principle of merit is the guiding principle in both worlds. Furthermore, he posed that the principles of rationalization applicable for work-life – time planning, bureaucracy, procedures – are adapted in sports, especially in structuring and measuring training efforts and performance. While able to plan these activities with relative freedom in contrast to the sphere of work, the commoditization of individual performance on the market is also apt for the world of sports. Rigauer makes a case that work and sports are not separate systems of practice, but follow the same logic. One might raise the objection that these critiques of sports are mostly relevant for the realm of professional competitive sports. However, the pervasiveness of work-related criteria in society becomes clearer when approaching them as part of instrumental reason. Following Adorno's essay on *Freizeit* (Leisure or Free Time, 1969), non-work activities are quantified and measured against their usefulness, not necessarily identical with criteria of productivity, but as a means to an end. William J. Morgan says: "Leisure becomes a repository for satisfying social needs unmet within the everyday context of labor. In so doing, it is absorbed within the realm of purposive reason, in which the reproduction of the capacity to labor becomes its central task" (Morgan 1988: 816).

Sports and other leisure activities are, thus, less means in and for themselves, but are mediated by the logic of instrumentality. The arguments that sports are beneficial for health, contribute to fitness, enjoyment and conviviality, have a compensatory function for an otherwise regulated life, or are distinctive of a specific class or group that all fall under this logic: "Sport extends social domination, according to Adorno, by incorporating instrumental praxis within itself. In so doing, sport becomes an after-image of work, a mere prolongation of production" (Morgan 1988: 817). Similarly, Habermas (one of whose students was Rigauer) speaks of the significance of work behavior in the sphere of leisure as "suspensive leisure time behavior" (Habermas 1958, cit. in Rigauer 1969: 7). The underlying paradox is that the increased availability of leisure in modern society – as opposed to earlier eras – increases and does not diminish the importance of norms and values from the sphere of work, be they principles of merit based on competition or other social factors. Thus, it seems that the pervasiveness of sports in society is, at the same time, the pervasiveness of instrumental reason in other forms.

Sportivity as Distinction, Distinct Cyclists

The "usefulness" of sports is also exemplified by its contribution to the formation of social and cultural identities, as has been illustrated by studies on the "transferability" of qualities from the sport to the work place (Kay & Laberge 2002). Such studies illustrate the role of sport as a means of distinction alongside its expected other positive effects. Comparable to the work of Elias and Dunning (1984), Bourdieu stresses that the profits of distinction promote some sports over others (1986). The argument is that sports such as tennis or golf carry a greater potential for reputation than other disciplines, and are thus preferred for their ability to create exclusivity and distinction. Moreover, Bourdieu posits that the choice of sport closely connects the perceived benefits of practice with certain lifestyles. Contingent on economic as well as on cultural capital, practicing sport is a relevant decision in the nexus of understandings of class specifics and identity formation.

Applying the concept of distinction to the realm of sports, this extension allows for two things: firstly, it gives a deeper insight into the modalities under which certain types of sport can be successful in historical contexts, and into how sports are carried out depending on ascriptions by different groups. The promotion and later demotion of cycling in the rise of modern society is an example of the centrality of changing sociocultural configurations for the practice of sports. The success of cycling as a recreational sport hinges on value ascriptions, so that, for example, a competitive motive in cycling can be both a stigma and an accolade, depending on historical conditions and on the groups of actors involved. As will be shown below, this holds true for current developments in cycling as well. It includes the forms or arrangements of practice in a social and a physical or bodily way. The social aspect of sports practices involves the composition of participants (members of an exclusive club, workers, amateurs, or professionals), the environment (a closed race track, public roads), norms of conduct (timed races, slow-paced ride), and appearance (clothing, equipment).

The physical aspect of practice makes up the second way in which the concept of distinction enriches an analysis of sports. It allows for a closer view of the body and body techniques, involving the "stylization" of life in conceptualizing the "body as an end in itself" (Bourdieu 1986: 589). One dimension of the body is its functionality, fitness and form being the prevalent indicators. Fitness and well-being have become substantial values in the modern and post-Fordist society (Graf 2013), and are pursued for their perceived instrumental benefits for health and productivity and promoted by the "fitness industry." In search of distinction, fitness or getting fit functions not as activity for the sake of activity, but as leisure activity for superordinate goals, such as identity formation, self-presentation or transfer-effects of enhanced performance within the frameworks of a "body boom" (Meuser 2004). Knowledge about "doing fitness" is a vital aspect of this trend that has been described by Bourdieu as the fragmentation of exercises, each directed at fulfilling a specific function. The myriad of advice books, periodicals and how to-manuals on the internet are a vivid demonstration of how meticulously the analysis of training routines proceeds to find the optimal, time-efficient and healthiest way of becoming or staying fit, including adjustments catering to trends of, for example, muscularity ("strong is beautiful") or skinniness ("slim is beautiful").

Following a rationalization of sports, a huge range of gadgets and platforms are available to gather, analyze and translate data to measure and improve performance in cycling, using diverse quantifying variables: heart rate, lung capacity, glycogen levels, lactate concentration, watt output, calories, speed, duration, distance, cadence, form, perceived intensity, repetitions, body fat, weight, or steps. These variables are measured against constructions of normalcy (body-mass indices, average power output) and scaled into categories (aerobic and anaerobic activity, power and heart rate zones, endurance and explosive strength) guiding and structuring training standards. Training efforts are thus increasingly rationalized against the backdrop of both their transferability and adaptability to other aspects of everyday life, the expected effect of particular workouts,

and the formation of identities along the lines of lifestyle and constructions of normal practice. Fitness and being fit is subject to scrutinizing quantification of guiding indicators, allowing for comparisons not only against oneself in performance improvement, but also against more abstract reference points.[3]

Another dimension of the body that plays an important role in fitness and sportivity trends – aesthetics – has gained new significance. The visual representation of the body is no longer limited to surface appearances, but includes non-apparent and invisible characteristics of the body as well. The transformation of bodies as a resource for creating meaning and the body as a relatively stable "projection surface" for identities (Hitzler 2002) is, as training and race data is made more and more transparent via internet platforms, lists of results or oral exchange, connected to "deep tissue." Enabled by detailed body knowledge, the shaping of bodies goes deeper than body fat, muscle definition or posture. Somatic reactions, heart rate, the flow of red blood cells, or twitch modalities of muscle fibers have become distinctive qualities even for recreational athletes. Thus, disciplining the body entails and requires the reflexive management of physical features beyond appearance. Specific aesthetic configurations are also important: sport-specific standards of muscle composition have been added to more general images of fit and healthy bodies. The pronounced muscular upper body that conventionally evokes connotations of strength and fitness, for example, is devalued in the sport of cycling as it is not performance- and output-oriented: The weight of muscles less needed for cycling is seen as a disadvantage, which prompted a recreational cyclist to seriocomically bemoan that he has to carry his biceps' weight up a climb.

Distinction via physical attributes within sports is – unsurprisingly – sport-specific, and it expands to residues which have not for long been thought to be accessible to processes of rationalization, quantification and aestheticization. Along with social arrangements of practice, they are a powerful means for the shaping of identities via sports, and stretch to divergent cultural patterns. They contribute to the accumulation of social capital in training, competition or urban events by reinforcing and representing social values, as Berking and Neckel (1993) have shown for the role of individuality in urban marathon events.

A more general and broadly applicable social value is "sportivity." While it has long since been identified as a guiding principle in modern society (Kaschuba 1989), its pervasiveness has drastically intensified over the last two decades. Nowadays, the percentage of regularly active sportive citizens has risen to – depending on the study – 70 percent to 80 percent doing sport at least once a week (TdW 2005). 28 percent are members of organized sports clubs, with gradual yearly increases (DOSB 2007, 2011, 2012; Grupe & Krüger 2007: 167), but with the prognosis of decline due to demographic trends (Steinbach & Hartmann 2007). Sportivity varies based on socioeconomic factors: Market research and surveys corroborate the observation that people highly active in sports for the most part originate in households with high net incomes and education levels (AWA 2009); older people or those with lower education levels are most likely not to be involved in sports at all.[4] The "typical" recreational athlete is male, white, in his late-thirties, and has a high income (Hartmann-Tews 1996; Humphreys & Ruseki 2009; TdW 2005) – this holds true for cyclists as well (AWA 2009). A survey of participants at a 2012 Jedermann race in Göttingen puts the average athlete at 42, with a high education level and good income. While the number of female participants is increasing, it is still marginal. Only 13 percent of participants for the Göttingen event were female; the numbers for other races are even smaller (interview with BDR, June 17, 2013).

Estimations put the yearly expenditure for age-group triathletes at approximately 2,750 euros (Wicker, Prinz & Weimar 2013), and one can assume that the expenditure figures for road cyclists are lower, yet comparable. The price of road bikes contributes especially to the high costs of the sport, with entry-level bikes starting at 900 euros and high-end "halo bikes" costing well over 10,000 euros. Cycling shoes, helmets, glasses, and other items of clothing add to the costs. This illustrates the influence of consumption patterns in sports where lightweight car-bon-fiber road bikes with electronic gears constitute objectified cultural capital and the choice of gear has differentiating signal effects. The "commodification of the cycle as an object" (Cox 2008: 10) is part of larger shifts in road cycling, related to consumption patterns, practices of self-presentation and event structure: "Road cycling is being relegitimised as an activity for certain groups of social elites, with echoes of the ways in which the earliest cycle clubs acted as opportunities for social display of values and disposable wealth" (ibid.).

Such shifts in value attribution or changing patterns of practice and presentation in cycling as a mass and recreational sport are linked to social paradigms of fitness and performance, pointing to cycling's role for processes of distinction and prompting inquiries into the reasons for phenomena such as huge sporting events, high degrees of organization of cycling competitions, or heavily structured and rationalized ways of doing sports. Part of the efforts to approach these areas have been, for a long time, attempts to create typologies and to segment sports participants into useful categories, guided mainly by motives for recreational athletes. Kaschuba differentiates between five commonplace motivational complexes: body ideals and aesthetics, health, communicative functions of sports, sensual experience, and performance (Kaschuba 1989: 164–165). These have been shown to be "standard" and consistent motives for sports activities in numerous studies by sports science, insurance companies or public administration over the last three decades. More focused analyses in marketing research try to detect "target groups," arriving at segmentations such as "serious pursuers," "sport lovers," and "socializers;" or "healthy joggers," "social competitors," "actualized athletes," and "devotees" (Wicker et al. 2012). For cycling, a BDR-initiated survey of interviewees having ridden any bike in the last six months distinguishes "health-oriented" (30 percent) from "socially oriented recreational cyclists" (27 percent), "purpose-oriented rationalists" (24 percent) and "involved athletes" (19 percent). The governing body was anticipating the first three categories, but expressed their surprise at the high number of "competitive recreational athletes:"

The comparably smallest, yet numerically surprisingly large segment with 19% are the involved athletes. This group – for the most part individualists – rides fast and sport-oriented on purpose to exert themselves. Professional athletes serve as role models. Top-quality equipment is highly valued.[5]

Given the prevailing definitions of mass and recreational sports in contrast to professional sports, it is no wonder the results of the survey, conducted to align the BDR's profile and services with the new needs of cyclists, were met with disbelief: Cycling as leisure is, according to long-standing paradigms, disconnected from the sphere of competitiveness and performance-orientation. While the trend of rationalizing and quantifying sports efforts for instrumental reasons is rhetorically easily accessible, the notion of competitiveness in hobby sports is still comparatively marginal. Looking closer at current processes in road cycling, I will argue in the following that the argumentative declaration of competitiveness is to some degree taboo. Competitive motives are veiled both by value attributions to non-professional road-cycling as non-competitive and by associated discursive registers. Competitive motives find their expression in micro aspects and in reflexive habitual patterns which often evade categorization, and relational and layered motives – in contrast to explicit statements of competitiveness – are not overt and make no direct reference to underlying instrumental or rationalized principles.

Cycling as Leisure and Competition

How do these processes materialize in German recreational road cycling, and in how far does performance-orientation and competition influence the structure of road racing in Germany? Similar to most other countries, road cycling in Germany is divided into three sections. At the top, paid professional cyclists[6] race in professional teams, with UCI ProTeams (such as the former Team Telekom) as the top tier, UCI Professional Continental Teams as the middle tier and UCI Continental Teams – where riders have contracts, but are not necessarily paid

– as the lowest tier *équipes*. This classification determines at which races teams are allowed to start, so that ProTeams have the right to race high-profile international events, such as the Tour de France or the Vuelta a España, Professional Continental Teams have to hope for invitations or wildcards for these World Tour races, and Continental Teams are limited to lower profile races.

The second level is for amateur riders. Cyclists have to be members of clubs approved by the respective national governing body (the BDR in Germany) in order to obtain a license which enables them to take part in amateur races. Amateur riders are typically unpaid, but can receive material support, such as bikes and a cycling kit, or be compensated for travel and accommodation expenses, et cetera. There are three performance categories available for amateur riders:[7] A, B and C. Riders must start with a C license – commonly viewed as the entrance to performance-oriented mass sport – and have to achieve either a win or five top-ten placements in order to get into the next higher category, and keep proving their performance not to be relegated.

Hobby cyclists make up the third level, that of mass and recreational sports. Typically, they do not hold one of the three license categories, nor do they participate in races – at least, this is the long-lasting expectation held by sports organizations and other institutions involved in cycling administration and policy. So-called Radtourenfahrten (RTF, cycling tours), biking excursions or cycle marathons are the classic formats available for hobby riders, with a focus not on performance but, as the BDR puts it, rather on the "contact with the environment (mostly nature), seeing and experiencing" (DSB 1976: 23), the social dimension of doing sports, "fun and joy," and the benefits for health and well-being: "The appetite is good, the sleep deep, and the self-confidence grows" (ibid.: 33). While cycling tours can involve score cards and tokens of appreciation, such as special jerseys for avid riders, an element of competitiveness is generally denied:

As a matter of principle, the spirit of competition in mass and recreational sports is to be rejected, it belongs to the realm of competitive sports. ... [The comparison of performance] cannot be eliminated, as it is a natural component of life. ... We do not support these aspects, but they cannot be prevented. (Ibid.: 23)

What Rigauer calls "bourgeois romanticist tendencies" (1969: 81), that is the ideological transfiguration of sports as part of a distinct leisure sphere in contrast to work-life, finds its expression in the normative claim that mass sports should not be competitive or involve performance comparisons. Indeed, this claim goes back to the beginnings of the sport in the early nineteenth century where competitiveness was discouraged and frowned upon. However, this interpretation of mass and recreational cyclists as noncompetitive actors with motives mostly unrelated to agonal principles has been challenged, and the spirit of competitiveness has been, as the quote above shows, an integral element of the sport from the beginning. Notwithstanding the rejection of competitive aspects in recreational cycling by sports associations, they are present at the level of practice. However, the perception of competition-free recreational sports is not just a discursive strategy, but an expression of a larger ideological configuration that posits a conceptual distinction between work and leisure.

There have been races with time-keeping open for cyclists without licenses for some time now, but the trend of big Jedermann races with a large number of participants is relatively new. In 1996, the first edition of the Hamburg Cyclassics, a professional race of the UCI's World Tour series, introduced two courses of 50 and 160 kilometers for age-group cyclists. A total of 2,400 riders took up the challenge, and, 17 years later, the 2013 edition of the Jedermann race has over 20,000 participants. In 2006, the T-Mobile Cycling Tour as the "first and only overall series of race events" for "ambitioned cyclists"[8] included the Cyclassics as one of around twenty races, building on the popularity of the sport. Two years later, when Telekom stepped down from all sponsorship activities in cycling following the doping scandal around Ullrich and others, the tour was discontinued. How-

ever, demands for a race series for recreational cyclists persisted, leading to the founding of the German Cycling Cup (GCC), a coordinated effort by the BDR and an initiative of cycle race promoters (the Verband Deutscher Radrennveranstalter). In 2008, nine races were part of the series, and in 2013, participants can score points in a total of fourteen races, mostly offering a choice between short and long distances. The Göttingen-based Tour d'Energie, an appendage of a former pro race like the Cyclassics, started with 1,062 participants on a 72 kilometer course and is now host to close to 3,000 cyclists on 46 and 100 kilometer courses.

The popularity of the series is illustrated by the number of participants, the range of sponsors, a dedicated online-publication,[9] and foremost, a number of almost professionally organized teams with high budgets and performance potentials that exceed the former level of ambitioned cyclists, causing worries for the BDR as the national governing body:

The Jedermann races have reached a stage that needs supervision like competitive sports. By now, there are German championships with doping tests, leader boards for all categories, well-sponsored teams with partially big financial budgets and professional support. The end to this boom is unforeseeable. The statistics for last year shows 50,000 starters for the German Cycling Cup alone. (BDR 2013: 24)

Despite the regulation that riders licensed in the top two categories of the BDR are not allowed to start at such races, the performance level is very high. In some teams, bi-annual training camps are held, and riders have extremely high amounts of training and equipment similar to professionals.

For amateur riders, a 16 percent decline of licensed riders over the last years (BDR 2013: 72) can be observed, prompting the BDR to give warnings against the death of the "decades-long proven A/B and C system of categories and their regulations" (ibid.: 24). Cases of former amateur-category racers discarding their A and B licenses in order to be able to participate in Jedermann races have been reported (BDR interview, FAZ 2012b). The rise of Jedermann races, in contrast to amateur racing, is largely attributed to the attractiveness of the new format:

> The atmosphere is totally different. As a Jedermann, you have a fantastic atmosphere and a huge fenced off racecourse; as an amateur, you drive sixty times around the church tower or through an industrial zone without any spectators. (Interview with a participant in FAZ 2012b)

There is a general worry on the part of the BDR about the impact that Jedermann races and related processes have on the conventional structures of recreational road cycling in Germany:

> It is also recognizable that cycle tours are increasingly used by many performance-oriented athletes to train for participation in Jedermann races that spring up like mushrooms. Sadly, reckless behavior, such as jumping red lights … of some groups has to be noted in some cases. … It should be argued that they are not bike races… (BDR 2013: 23)

The concurrence of different developments is noteworthy: There is an increasing interest in the format of competitive races with top cyclists able to ride on the level of higher-ranking amateurs; even ex-professional riders are part of the field. The number of sponsored teams competing for the leader board is steadily growing, attracting more well-trained riders and providing incentives to improve in order to secure a spot on one of these teams. In any case, the level of performance in Jedermann races is remarkable. A high number of participants are eager to compete for good placements and to measure their performance against others, contrary to the BDR's insistence on the subordination of competitive motives in recreational cycling. Prior to the rise of Jedermann races, amateur-level racing would have been a venue to cater to this need for competition. Simultaneously, the eventization of non-professional cycle races – following a more general trend towards big events (Betz, Hitzler & Pfadenhauer 2011; Hepp & Vogelgesang 2003; Hitzler 2011; Klein 2004) – attracts a diverse range of participants from all levels of performance and with different motivations to take part. As there are also significant differences in skills, knowledge and experience related to riding such races, organizers and participants alike have remarked the growing conflicts in these races. Here, processes of professionalization meet processes of eventization and inclusion:[10] The aim of organizers is to attract large numbers of participants to make the events economically feasible and profitable. This leads to a situation where occasional cyclists, avid beginners and well-trained sponsored riders meet "at high speed," causing partly dangerous situations when riders overestimate their skills or overexert themselves and ride "in the red" with potentially dangerous consequences. The dangers of this development are extensively discussed in online fora and on Facebook,[11] prompting some organizers to reflect on possibilities to separate highly ambitioned riders looking to score points for the German Cycling Cup from cyclists portrayed as "recreational" or "looking for a good time." Initial developments like invitation only events for top GCC riders or changes in course planning[12] show an awareness both of the increasing focus on winning as a potential for the format and the conflicts which can spring up from its popularity.

The concurrence of these developments is also a "clash" of different cultural patterns of practice. There has been a shift from recreational events like cycle tours or small timed races with – in comparison to current races – few participants, to highly competitive races with pelotons (the main field of a race) of a couple of hundred riders in a group, team tactics, breakaways, and bunch sprints. This involves the transposition of competitive patterns to performance patterns initially dominated by other cultural patterns like social or recreational rides. The popularization of performance principles (Grupe & Krüger 2007: 309ff.) in mass and recreational sports is critical for such shifts. Competitive motives are, it seems, becoming more and more pervasive in non-professional sports activities, and find their expression in popular sports events. This development is largely attributed to the significance and centrality of the principle of merit in modern society. Its manifestation in big urban events, new consumption patterns, and marketing and sponsoring activities are regularly ascribed to the expansion of neoliberal paradigms to all aspects of everyday life (Andrews & Silk 2012). Drawing from the deliberations above, I would argue that this account misses an important aspect. Instrumental reason, as shown above, has been the driving force behind sports activities, both professional and recreational, from very early on. This includes elements of competitiveness and performance orientation, not only in team sports. While further inquiry is needed, especially a focused historical ethnography tracing the development of competitive motives and semantics in the sport of cycling from its emergence in the late-nineteenth century in Germany, the literature available suggests that they have always been parts of the sport (cf. especially Rabenstein 1996; Gronen & Lemke 1987). Furthermore, it is crucial to distinguish the guiding principles from their manifestations. The individualization of performance – interrelated to larger social trends of individualization in a risk society (Beck 1986) – and accordingly, a performance orientation in the private sports sphere favored a relatively intraindividual comparison of strength, speed or stamina, not visible on the surface like relative interindividual comparisons such as races. However, this does not mean that instrumental principles were nonexistent in these private spheres. A constriction of economic influence on complex life worlds to concrete and tacit economic principles misses the finer gradients of extra-work activities not apparently linked to work-life – as Habermas has shown, not even suspensive or compensatory leisure time behaviors are external to these principles. Rather, the current developments in road cycling should be viewed as realizations of profound principle in the context of new configurations of practice.[13]

Quantification, Rationalization, and Transparency

What then are – apart from the dictum of economization or neoliberalization – the factors that have led to the genesis and success of Jedermann races in Germany? There are a number of interdependent "enablers" vital to the current situation in road cycling, both in racing and training. While I will focus here on their influence on road cycling, they are certainly also potent in other areas of sports and everyday life.

The first cluster of such enablers consists of new techniques in the realms of quantification and rationalization. An increasing number of tools and gadgets are on the market allowing performance measurement, tracking and analysis. They are able to record performance indicators such as strength, endurance or recuperativeness. These techniques stretch from very basic things, such as measuring weight or speed via scales and simple bike-attached speedometers, to sophisticated devices, such as quantifying leg-specific power output via power meters. Power meters, coming from professional sports, are highly expensive diagnostic tools attached to the cranks of a bike to monitor the wattage produced by a cyclist. In combination with performance tests, such as spirometry (measuring lung capacity) or lactate measurements, power zones and anaerobic thresholds are analyzed to determine training and race recommendations.[14] Training plans are then structured aided by these power zones, trying to prevent "junk miles" (that is training miles outside recommended power or heart rate zones). Recently, more affordable power meters have been introduced onto the market, making them a more viable alternative to popular heart rate monitors. The supply of performance diagnostics, position and mobility analyses as a service, providing individualized training plans even for recreational cyclists, builds on these data. Training diaries on a range of online platforms help one to follow the specific schedules aligned to the goals for the season. Less refined versions of training analyses include ready-made training plans that can be used individually with the help of diagnostic tools such as heart rate monitors. Furthermore, tests in cycling publications and online fora inform readers about new "tech" – equipment and clothing – and its potential to increase performance by reducing drag or friction. The quantification of performance is, moreover, enabled by GPS location services, recording the courses ridden by cyclists and creating "segments," for example a hill or a time trial course. Comparing one's performance to earlier rides becomes effortless, as times are measured automatically for the course or segment given. Former instances of measuring course performance have been – besides races – so-called *Stoppomats*: Installed at the foot and peak of climbs, a cyclist would fill out a card at the foot of the climb with his name and punch it into the *Stoppomat* which would print a time stamp on it. At the top of the climb, one would punch it in again and deposit the card into a box. The cards would then be collected at regular intervals and leader boards be published in local cycling magazines. Nowadays, results from *Stoppomats* are posted online. Power meters, diagnostics and training plans closely follow the logics of rationalization, including references to and disputes about scientific studies or citing the training methods of professionals as guiding patterns for the training of recreational cyclists. They are linked to fitness and sportivity paradigms that have emerged over the course of the last decades, stressing the importance of fit and healthy bodies. Furthermore, these tools facilitate the more direct and substantiated mapping of instrumental principles to performance-oriented goals. Thus, these new quantifying instruments have the enabling potential for optimizing and perfect training schedules, even in the realm of non-professional cycling. In this regard, the trickle-down effects from professional sports as well as the mediation of training paradigms through bike-specific publications and media are central factors for this development.

Closely connected to the techniques of quantification and rationalization are new techniques of transparency. Data acquired from heart rate monitors, cadence and speed sensors, and power meters, as well as training logs, are increasingly uploaded to a range of online platforms and made publicly available.

So-called Winter Trophies ("Winterpokal") rank riders or teams of riders according to the duration of training over the winter months; on Strava,[15] the data of single rides – including speed, heart rate, (estimated) power, VAM (*velocità ascensionale media*, average ascent speed), and time – can be measured against past efforts as well as other cyclists having ridden the same course. The results are virtual leader boards segmented by age group, gender and weight class. Analogous to professional races, the fastest riders of a climb or segment are designated King or Queen of the Mountain (KOM/QOM) – when they lose a KOM, an e-mail is automatically sent to encourage them to win it back. Outside of training, race results are posted online and in leader boards of race series, such as the German Cycling Cup or the Jedermann portal,[16] creating rankings for all riders and teams participating in Jedermann races, based on points gained in each competition. Transparency also involves knowledge about training methodology and practice, for example the newest trends in professional training, flexibility or strength exercises, technique, and equipment. While many riders will not use the full extensive functionality of online platforms or extremely expensive training devices, the "base layer" of transparency techniques – comparing one's own performance with the performances of others – causes an expansion of the digital dimension of cycling, having a direct impact on competitiveness and how rides are experienced.

This is linked to the third cluster concerning the connection of technical aspects with social factors. Enabled by techniques of quantification and transparency, the individualization of performance – both in training and in races – can draw from virtual proximities of riders and their efforts. As a result, athletes in mass and recreational sports have an increasing number of reference points for their performance. One is no longer limited to monitoring one's own performances, but one can also see how one stacks up against other riders in terms of results or speed. This leads to new relationalities and, consequently, to a networked or relational re-individualization as a cultural pattern of performance: the individualization of competitiveness, that is that personal efforts are measured and improvement is aspired to on a personal level, is coupled with new techniques, massively expanding the possibilities to relate oneself to others without necessarily being in direct contact. While this re-individualization does not mimic professional competitive interpretations, it involves a stratification of competitiveness with divergent points of reference: the self, and different performance or age groups as the other. Online leader boards and virtual KOM classifications on Strava are examples of the potential of putting various people into competition without them having to know each other. KOM notifications and leader boards are able to create directed competitive stimuli by putting efforts into relation with each other. Thus, the digital tools available to mass and recreational cyclists create new competitive patterns based on already existing developments, such as the popularization and individualization of performance principles, and the rationalization and quantification of sports, as well as everyday life. What can be observed is both a stabilization and continuation of these relations and patterns. Jedermann race series continue and expand and online dimensions of the sport are extended, both on online platforms gaining new "social features" and on social networking sites.

However, these competitive patterns are still relatively unstable or fragile. An expression of this fragility is the fact that there is mostly no "immediacy" or directness to competitive motives, but rather a layered approach. As interviews with recreational cyclists participating in Jedermann races have shown, there are both stratification and temporality attached to competitiveness as well as its explication. The stratification finds its expression in a sequential layering of motives: Recreational motives, such as staying healthy and fit, losing weight and enjoying the sport, are often foregrounded, while overtly instrumental motives, such as compensation for stressful work or private life, are subordinated. However, they are – closely linked to the findings of Elias and Dunning – widespread among cyclists, who argue that the relaxation from cycling helps them in their busy work or personal lives. Competitive dimensions, that is improving one's performance for

the sake of performance, riding faster than other riders or achieving a good placement in races, are often less directly communicated or only formulated ex post. Both the fragility of the competitive pattern in recreational sports and the discursive subordination of competitive motives as part of the dichotomy between work and leisure favor the underemphasis of competition. This is, of course, not a stratification of motives that can be generalized for all cyclists. There are a number of identifiable types of riders along the lines of recreational cyclists who initially deny competitive motives; cyclists highlighting their individual improvement as the primary goal; riders clearly competitive but stressing that their expectations are low in view of their own performance and other, better riders; and highly ambitioned riders aiming at achieving top results in races. Segmentations have their limit, and this is especially the case for segmented motivations in recreational sports. Creating a typology of three or four different athlete types for marketing purposes might make sense, as Wicker et al. (2012) argue for the triathlon. However, such typologies are not sufficient for an ethnological analysis, most notably because of the stratification of motives. When further inquiries are made, specific competitive motives are regularly communicated in addition to recreational instrumental motives, even if a competitive dimension is denied initially: "Yes, of course, one tries to ride faster than other riders one knows on a climb," a cyclist stressing her noncompetitive aspirations in the sport stated (interview with C., June 14, 2013). The account of another cyclist who recognized one of his team members in a race who started the race faster than him:

> When I saw him, I have to say, it is not really nice to say, I know, but I was happy that I caught him. … I take other riders of my club as a comparison, and my aim is, of course, to be as fast as them or better. … Well, I know it is not possible, but I want to take a podium place in one of these races one day. (Interview with J., September 12, 2013)

More ambitioned riders explicate their competitive motivations more clearly and include specific goals in their formulation: "My aim is to move from the top 20 of my age group to the top 10 in the next season" (interview with D., September 10, 2013).

One important aspect of the formulation of competitive motives hinges on what one might call immersion: Relations to other riders in combination with performance and potential can be created to measure one's performance not only in terms of speed, time or abstract ranking, but also with specific reference to single riders. This results in joy about being faster than another rider in the sprint finish or excitement that one is able to "follow the wheel" of a competitor up a climb. The notion of relative expectation horizons is vital here, as it enables new relationalities between different athletes: "Well, I don't know, I have no experience, no horizon of expectation of how to rate my performance" (interview with J., September 12, 2013).

Relatively narrow expectation horizons closely relate to how competitive motives are formulated, and techniques of transparency and quantification are important enablers creating denser networks of performance knowledge, resulting in cyclists' abilities to relate to each other's performance. There is, of course, an amplifying effect of existing cultural practices and competitive patterns, leading to persistent influences of competitive stimuli and cyclists, for example in how training efforts are structured, how race seasons are approached or which expectations riders have. As Jedermann races grow more popular and more and more riders participate in these events, competitive motives and patterns gain importance (the diametrical opposite being that an increasing number of riders shy away from highly competitive groups and choose to ride at the back, as a race organizer observed). The appropriation of discursive registers – the "vocabulary" of ambitioned cyclists – including argumentative strategies and communicative ways to make sense of race efforts, forms another distinct element of competitiveness in recreational sports. Besides registers from professional sports, including expressions like "bridging a gap" or "leeching" (riding in the slipstream of other cyclists without contributing to pace making), the elicitation of stratification is a remarkable feature of discourse.

Related to the fragility of competitiveness in recreational cycling as a cultural pattern, expressions of competitive motives are, for the most part, coupled with mitigating phrases. Outright statements of ambition ("I want to win", "I want to be better than him") are much less frequent than remarks pointing out the relativity of one's performance ("I want to improve my own performance/to keep my current form", "It would be nice to be able to ride with the top group") – though further inquiry into the discursive manifestations of competitiveness is required, direct and strong utterances of competitive ambitions still seem to be, in contrast to professional sports, less encouraged in spite of recent developments towards performance orientation. Instead, what can be observed is the relationality of competitiveness as participants construct isolated standards of comparison regarding their performance ("Can I improve my time?", "Can I beat my training partner?"). In this respect, the long-standing normative dictum that recreational cycling should not be competitive seems to prevail here in a modified form, favoring relative instead of absolute performance comparisons. An intriguing observation in this context is that, in order to be successful, top riders in Jedermann races need to adapt their work schedules heavily to their extensive training efforts, creating the need to justify such an emphasis on the sport. At a certain point, the intensive pursuit of cycling with highly rationalized and structured training regimen evades the frames for interpreting recreational cycling. The justifications for such efforts heavily draw from the principle of merit in professional sports, illustrating its pervasiveness in its non-professional counterpart.

The temporality of competitive motives is another important aspect, albeit in a more ephemeral fashion: The atmosphere of big race events, seeing a teammate or a known competitor in a race can function as a "trigger" or competitive stimulus. This points to the necessity of observing road cycling as performance; strong cases have been made for extensive ethnographies of bodily practices and sports as performance (Honer 2011), and the same holds true for road cycling and competitiveness. Ephemeral competitive stimuli are accessible by interviews as well, but direct access depends both on direct ethnographic encounters as well as on coincidence: One revealing episode during a Jedermann race in Hanover placed the ethnographer in a small group trying to bridge a gap to the field at the front at the race, with one of the riders swerving out of the Belgian tourniquet (a formation where several riders take turn at the front and then fall back into slipstream) and bringing down the next closest rider. As it turned out, the two were husband and wife, producing an argument right after they had checked for bodily or technical harm: "Why did you do that?", the husband asked, alluding to her apparently riding "in the red" and overexerting herself, thus – according to him – not being able to properly control her bike and causing the accident. "This was the first time we have been so close to the top group, and I wanted to stay in contact with them!", she exclaimed; the stimulus of seeing the front of the race at such a close distance caused them to accept risks, as they explained to me while we were standing – unharmed – at the side of the road. Indeed, this is a common critique of Jedermann races based on experiences of accidents and crashes over the last couple of years. Riders are caught up in the moment and try to ride harder than they can, looking for gaps where no gaps exist or riding faster than they are used to. Competitive patterns are, in that regard, very influential.

Conclusion

Both stratification and temporality of competitiveness illustrate intermingled motivational spheres as well as the limits of segmentation. The pervasiveness of competitiveness as a cultural pattern does not only apply to those cyclists voicing direct ambitions, but also to other athletes seemingly less interested in producing a good performance. The popularity and possibility of big urban events, the increase of transparency and availability of data and knowledge, the increasing quantification and rationalization of recreational sports: these are vital enablers for the emergence of new competitive patterns in mass and recreational sports. Techniques, knowledge, transparency, and new forms of social rela-

tions are important aspects of this configuration; in their convergence with trends towards urban events, they bring about new constellations of competitive performances, such as Jedermann races including a professionalization of ambitioned hobby cyclists. Thus, I would argue that the phenomena of these races and new forms of competitive patterns in mass and recreational sports should not be constricted to the increasing influence of economic (or neoliberal) principles on life worlds, but that they have been facilitated by the concurrence of the developments outlined above, amplifying – but not replacing or creating – existing cultural patterns of rationalization, quantification, and competitiveness.

This article, viewing sports as an integral part of everyday culture, inquired into road cycling as a cultural performance. It mapped the crucial dimensions and underlying processes which an ethnological research program on new and emerging patterns of sport activity in modern society will have to take into account. Many of the elements outlined here are efficacious for other realms of everyday life as well, but manifest conspicuously in the realm of cycling. The quantification of the self and of performance, the rationalization of practice – both in its meaning of training and action – and the stratification of competitive motives point beyond cycling to much more pervasive sociocultural processes demanding further research.

There are a number of aspects upon which I have not touched in this article, but that seem crucial for further inquiry into cycling as a mass and recreational sport in light of current developments. One of these aspects is doping in recreational cycling. Doping in the history of professional cycling has been extensively thematized (cf. Houlihan 2002). While most of the literature on doping in sports focuses on professional sports (Bette & Schimank 2000) or its potential negative influence on young athletes, newer studies have also started to problematize doping and substance abuse in mass sports (cf. Müller-Platz et al. 2006). The use of steroids in gyms (Kläber 2010) has been a popular example for the reach of doping into non-professional spheres. From caffeine, analgesics, asthma medication to over-the-counter NSAIDs (non-steroidal anti-inflammatory drugs, e.g. Ibuprofen) and finally to EPO (erythropoietin) or human growth hormones (HGH) – the range of substances used in mass sports (and everyday life; Robert Koch-Institut 2006, 2011) is huge, prompting officials to administer drug tests at the German Jedermann championship in 2012 and urban triathlon events in Germany. While there have been no known cases of doping in recreational road cycling in Germany yet, tests at the New York Gran Fondo in 2012 resulted in two hobby riders testing positive for EPO.[17] A survey of Swiss endurance events estimated that 5–10 percent of athletes in mass sports use NSAIDs to treat pain during races (Mahler 2001). Another recent study found high percentages of physical (13 percent) and cognitive (15.1 percent) doping among recreational triathletes in Germany (Dietz et al. 2013), suggesting a "general propensity to enhance" (ibid.: 8) rather than abusing substances for specific race goals. These findings fit the hypothesis of the pervasiveness of principles of self-quantification, rationalization and self-optimization, although further inquiry into this sensitive topic is needed.

Furthermore, and closely linked to pro-cycling where masculinity and heroism are highly valued while women's cycling is largely neglected by media, race organizers, sponsors and spectators, aspects of gender demand closer scrutiny. Jedermann races are predominantly occupied by men, but serve as a dense field of inquiry into gender issues as men and women currently start in the same races, causing disputes about safety and fairness. What are the reasons for the long-lasting under-representation of women in Jedermann races and recreational road cycling? On which levels do perceptions of rationalization, quantification and competitiveness differ based on gender differences, and how does this materialize in performance?

Lastly, the role of technology has been touched upon tangentially in this article, yet further ethnographic inquiry into the role of technology and bikes as objectified cultural capital, innovation, extension of the body, and – clearly – fetish is called for. The adaptation of new technology as well as the circu-lation of technological and scientific knowledge in the realm of cycling is closely linked to the ways in which road racing as competition is performed. Perspectives from science and technology studies present an opportunity to further conceptualize this interface between sports and technology and promise insights into the interaction between different forms of knowledge and action.

Notes

1 There had also been processes in the Weimar period linking physical exercises to rationalization and debates about a "human economy" (Dinçkal 2013).
2 The developments of the transformation of cycling in Germany from a historical perspective deserve far more attention than this article can provide.
3 This is linked to the "quantified self"-movement, where extensive data on the body is harnessed, processed and analyzed. See http://quantifiedself.com, accessed September 22, 2013.
4 See http://www.presseportal.de/print/2505640-aktuelle-umfrage-zum-umgang-mit-stress-im-job-ausgleich-theoretisch-beim.html, accessed September 22, 2013.
5 http://www.bdr-medienservice.de/index.php?id=518&thema=1752, accessed September 10, 2013. All translations from German to English by the author.
6 Formally, the distinction between professionals and amateurs was replaced by age categories in 1990, see http://www.uci.ch/Modules/BUILTIN/getObject.asp?MenuId=MTkzNg&ObjTypeCode=FILE&type=FILE&id=34033&LangId=1, accessed September 22, 2013.
7 http://www.rad-net.de/modules.php?name=html&f=disziplinen/kategorien.htm&menuid=107, accessed September 22, 2013.
8 http://breitensport.rad-net.de/aktuelles/2007/die-t-mobile-cycling-tour-geht-2007-in-die-zweite-runde.html, accessed September 22, 2013.
9 http://www.challenge-magazin.com, accessed September 22, 2013.
10 I am refererring to the notion of "inclusion" from sports studies as the process of including individuals in social subsystems like sports (cf. Hartmann-Tews 1996: 37).
11 https://www.facebook.com/groups /140043912701934/, accessed September 22, 2013.
12 The Bremen "Race of Champions" invited the top 100 men and top 40 women of the Jedermann scene for a race, see http://www.bremen-challenge.de/index.php?pid=276&state=page&action=default, accessed September 22, 2013.
13 Neckel (2008) shows a similar pervasive transposition of a "culture of success" to all aspects of society.
14 Such rationalization of riding and its manifestation in

professional races – riding at a determined wattage using a powermeter – has been critiqued for its lack of spontaneity or dullness in contrast to "instinctive" racing styles: see http://www.cyclingnews.com/news/nibali-its-a-huge-personal-satisfaction-to-win-tirreno-adriatico, accessed September 22, 2013.

15 http://www.strava.com, accessed September 22, 2013. There was a lawsuit against Strava following the death of a cyclist trying to beat a KOM on a descent. It was argued that Strava encouraged risky riding by creating leader boards and incentivizing riders to reclaim KOMs. The lawsuit has been dismissed. See http://velonews.competitor.com/2013/06/news/strava-wins-dismissal-of-civil-suit-over-berkeley-death_289714, accessed September 22, 2013.

16 For the GCC: https://service.acceptus.de/rennen/forms/sort.php?id=m&y=2013, accessed September 22, 2013. For the Jedermann-Portal: http://jedermann.rad-net.de/jedermannrangliste/, accessed September 22, 2013.

17 http://www.bikeradar.com/news/article/two-amteurs-test-positive-for-epo-at-gran-fondo-new-york-34711/, accessed September 22, 2013.

References

Adorno, T.W. 1969: Freizeit. In: T.W. Adorno (ed.), *Stichworte. Kritische Modelle 2*. Frankfurt a.M.: Suhrkamp, pp. 59.

Andrews, D.L. & M.L. Silk (eds.) 2012: *Sport and Neoliberalism: Politics, Consumption, and Culture*. Philadelphia: Temple University Press.

AWA 2009: *Allensbacher Markt- und Werbeträger-Analyse 2009*. Allensbach: Institut für Demoskopie Allensbach.

Bausinger, H. 1990: Die schönste Nebensache... Etappen der Sportbegeisterung. In: O. Grupe (ed.), *Kulturgut oder Körperkult? Sport und Sportwissenschaft im Wandel*. Tübingen: Attempto, pp. 3–21.

Bausinger, H. 2006: *Sportkultur*. Tübingen: Attempto.

BDR 2013: *Bundeshauptversammlung 23. März 2013 in Gelsenkirchen*. Jahresberichte 2012. Frankfurt: Bund Deutscher Radfahrer.

Beck, U. 1986: *Risikogesellschaft: Auf dem Weg in eine andere Moderne*. Frankfurt: Suhrkamp.

Berking, H. & S. Neckel 1993: Urban Marathon: The Staging of Individuality as an Urban Event. *Theory, Culture & Society* 10:4, 63–78.

Bernett, H. 1966: *Nationalsozialistische Leibeserziehung: Eine Dokumentation ihrer Theorie und Praxis*. Schorndorf: Hofmann.

Besnier, N. & S. Brownell 2012: Sport, Modernity, and the Body. *Annual Review of Anthropology* 41, 443–459.

Bette, K.-H. 1999: *Systemtheorie und Sport*. Frankfurt am Main: Suhrkamp.

Bette, K.-H. & U. Schimank 2000: Doping als Konstellationsprodukt. In: M. Gamper, J. Mühletaler & F. Reidhaar (eds.), *Doping: Spitzensport als gesellschaftliches Problem*. Zürich: Neue Züricher Zeitung Verlag, pp. 91–112.

Betz, G., R. Hitzler & M. Pfadenhauer (eds.) 2011: *Urbane Events*. Wiesbaden: VS-Verlag für Sozialwissenschaften.

Bourdieu, P. 1986: Historische und soziale Voraussetzungen modernen Sports. *Merkur* 39, 575–590.

Cachay, K. & A. Thiel 2000: *Soziologie des Sports: Zur Ausdifferenzierung und Entwicklungsdynamik des Sports der modernen Gesellschaft*. Weinheim: Juventa.

Cox, P. 2008: Class and Competition: The Gentrification of Sport Cycling. Paper given at the 5th Cycling and Society Symposium.

Dauncey, H. 2003: French Cycling Heroes of the Tour: Winners and Losers. In: H. Dauncey & G. Hare (eds.), *The Tour de France 1903–2003: A Century of Sporting Structures, Meanings and Values*. London: Frank Cass, pp. 175–202.

Dieckert, J. 2002: Freizeitsport in Deutschland. In: J. Dieckert & C. Wopp (eds.), *Handbuch Freizeitsport*. Schorndorf: Hofmann, pp. 69–100.

Dietz, P., R. Ulrich, R. Dalaker, H. Striegel, A.G. Franke, K. Lieb & P. Simon 2013: Associations between Physical and Cognitive Doping: A Cross-Sectional Study in 2,997 Triathletes. *PloS One* 8:11, 1–10.

Digel, H. 2012: Kulturen des Wettbewerbs im Sport. In: J. Starbatty, G. Vogt-Spira & J. Wertheimer (eds.), *Kultur des Wettbewerbs – Wettbewerb der Kulturen*. Stuttgart: Franz Steiner Verlag, pp. 69–100.

Dinçkal, N. 2013: „Sport ist die körperliche und seelische Selbsthygiene des arbeitenden Volkes": Arbeit, Leibesübungen und Rationalisierungskultur in der Weimarer Republik. *Body Politics* 1:1, 71–97.

DOSB 2007: *Demographische Entwicklung in Deutschland: Herausforderung für die Sportentwicklung*. Frankfurt: Deutscher Olympischer Sportbund.

DOSB 2011: *Mitgliederentwicklung im Sportverein: Bestandserhebungen und demographischer Wandel*. Frankfurt: Deutscher Olympischer Sportbund.

DOSB 2012: *Bestandserhebung 2012*. Frankfurt: Deutscher Olympischer Sportbund.

DSB 1976: *Leistungsvergleich und Wettkampf im Freizeit- und Breitensport*. Frankfurt: Deutscher Sportbund.

Elias, N. & E. Dunning 1984: Leisure in the Sparetime Spectrum. In: W. Hopf (ed.), *Sport im Zivilisationsprozess: Studien zur Figurationssoziologie*. Münster: Lit, pp. 145–151.

FAZ 2012a: *Raus aus dem Büro, rein ins Abenteur: Michael Ashelm*, November 25, 2012.

FAZ 2012b: *Jedermann ein Star: Michael Eder*, October 13, 2012.

Feddersen, A., S. Jacobsen & W. Maenning 2009: Sports Heroes and Mass Sports Participation: The (Double) Paradox of the "German Tennis Boom." *Hamburg Contemporary Economic Discussions* 29.

Gieseler, K. & J. Palm 1985: *Sport, Gesundheit, Wirtschaft:*

Breiten- und Freizeitsport in der Bundesrepublik Deutschland. Köln: Deutscher Instituts-Verlag.

Götz, I. 2013: Sensing Post-Fordist Work-Life: Recent Perspectives in the Ethnography of Work. *Ethnologia Europaea* 43:1, 68–87.

Graf, S. 2013: Leistungsfähig, attraktiv, erfolgreich, jung und gesund: Der fitte Körper in post-fordistischen Verhältnissen. *Body Politics* 1:1, 139–157.

Gronen, W. & W. Lemke 1987: *Geschichte des Radsports und des Fahrrades.* Hausham: Fuchs.

Grupe, O. & M. Krüger 2007: *Einführung in die Sportpädagogik.* Schorndorf: Hofmann.

Gugutzer, R. (ed.) 2006: *Body Turn: Perspektiven der Soziologie des Körpers und des Sports.* Bielefeld: Transcript.

Habermas, J. 1958: Soziologische Notizen zum Verhältnis von Arbeit und Freizeit. In: G. Funke (ed.), *Konkrete Vernunft: Festschrift für Erich Rothacker.* Bonn: Bouvier, pp. 219–231.

Hartmann-Tews, I. 1996: *Sport für alle!? Strukturwandel europäischer Sportsysteme im Vergleich: Bundesrepublik Deutschland, Frankreich, Großbrittanien.* Köln: Karl Hofmann Schorndorf.

Hepp, A. & W. Vogelgesang (eds.) 2003: *Populäre Events: Medienevents, Spielevents, Spaßevents.* Opladen: Leske & Budrich.

Hitzler, R. 1991: Ist Sport Kultur? *Zeitschrift für Soziologie* 20:6, 479–487.

Hitzler, R. 2002: Der Körper als Gegenstand der Gestaltung: Über physische Konsequenzen der Bastelexistenz. In: K. Hahn & M. Meuser (eds.), *Körperrepräsentationen: Die Ordnung des Sozialen und der Körper.* Konstanz: UVK, pp. 71–85.

Hitzler, R. 2011: *Eventisierung: Drei Fallstudien zum marketingstrategischen Massenspaß.* Wiesbaden: VS-Verlag für Sozialwissenschaften.

Honer, A. 2011: Lebensweltliche Ethnographie und das Phänomen Sport. In: A. Honer (ed.), *Kleine Leiblichkeiten: Erkundungen in Lebenswelten.* Wiesbaden: VS Verlag, pp. 75–88.

Houlihan, B. 2002: *Dying to Win: Doping in Sport and the Development of Anti-Doping Policy.* Strasbourg: Council of Europe Publishing.

Humphreys, B. & J. Ruseki 2009: The Economics of Participation and Time Spent in Physical Activity. University of Alberta, Department of Economics Working Paper No. 2009–09.

Husmann, R. & G. Krüger (eds.) 2002: *Ethnologie und Sport.* Frankfurt: Verlag für Interkulturelle Kommunikation.

Johler, R. 2003: In der Zwischenwelt der Kulturen: Volkskunde, Volksspiele und Sport. In: K. Maase & B.J. Warneken (eds.), *Unterwelten der Kultur: Themen und Theorien der volkskundlichen Kulturwissenschaft.* Köln: Böhlau, pp. 180–201.

Kaschuba, W. 1989: *Sportivität: Die Karriere eines neuen Leitwertes.* Sportwissenschaft 19:2, 154–171.

Kay, J. & S. Laberge 2002: The 'New' Corporate Habitus in Adventure Racing. *International Review for the Sociology of Sport* 37:1, 17–36.

Kläber, M. 2010: *Doping im Fitness-Studio: Die Sucht nach dem perfekten Körper.* Wiesbaden: Transcript.

Klein, G. 2004: Marathon, Parade und Olympiade: Zur Festivalisierung und Eventisierung der postindustriellen Stadt. *Sport und Gesellschaft* 3, 269–290.

Kurz, D. & K.D. Storck 1994: Breitensportentwicklung in Nordrhein-Westfalen. In: R. Winkels (ed.), *Bausteine der Breitensportentwicklung in Nordrhein-Westfalen: Materialien zum Sport in Nordrhein-Westfalen 40.* Frechen: Ritterbach, pp. 55–65.

Mahler, N. 2001: Medikamentenmissbrauch im Breitensport. *Therapeutische Umschau* 58:4, 226–231.

Meuser, M. 2004: Zwischen „Leibvergessenheit" und „Körperboom": Die Soziologie und der Körper. *Sport und Gesellschaft* 3, 192–218.

Morgan, W.J. 1988: Adorno on Sport: The Case of the Fractured Dialectic. *Theory and Society* 17, 813–838.

Müller-Platz, C., C. Boos & R.K. Müller 2006: *Doping beim Freizeit- und Breitensport: Gesundheitsberichterstattung des Bundes.* Heft 34. Berlin: Robert Koch-Institut.

Neckel, S. 2008: *Flucht nach vorn: Die Erfolgskultur der Marktgesellschaft.* Frankfurt am Main: Campus.

Palmer, C. 2002: Introduction: Anthropology and Sport. *Australian Journal of Anthropology* 13.3, 253–256.

Plessner, H. (1956)1997: Die Funktion des Sports in der industriellen Gesellschaft. In: V. Caysa (ed.), *Sportphilosophie.* Leipzig: Reclam, pp. 46–67.

Rabenstein, R. 1996: *Radsport und Gesellschaft: Ihre sozialgeschichtlichen Zusammenhänge in der Zeit von 1867 bis 1914.* Hildesheim: Weidmann.

Rigauer, B. 1969: *Sport und Arbeit: Soziologische Zusammenhänge und ideologische Implikationen.* Frankfurt am Main: Suhrkamp.

Robert Koch-Institut 2006: *Doping beim Freizeit- und Breitensport.* Berlin: Robert Koch-Institut.

Robert Koch-Institut 2011: *KOLIBRI: Studie zum Konsum leistungsbeeinflussender Mittel in Alltag und Freizeit.* Berlin: Robert Koch-Institut.

Schäfer, R. 2011a: *Militarismus, Nationalismus, Antisemitismus: Carl Diem und die Politisierung des bürgerlichen Sports im Kaiserreich.* Berlin.

Schäfer, R. 2011b: Carl Diem, der Antisemitismus und das NS-Regime. *Zeitschrift für Geschichtswissenschaft* 59, 252–263.

Steinbach, D. & S. Hartmann 2007: Demografischer Wandel und organisierter Sport: Projektionen der Mitgliederentwicklung des DOSB für den Zeitraum bis 2030. *Sport und Gesellschaft* 4:3, 223–242.

Tauschek, M. 2012: Wettbewerbskulturen: Eine kulturanthropologische Problemskizze. *Zeitschrift für Volkskunde* 108:2, 77–197.

Tauschek, M. 2013: Zur Kultur des Wettbewerbs: Eine Einführung. In: M. Tauschek (ed.), *Kulturen des Wettbewerbs: Formationen kompetitiver Logiken*. Münster: Waxman.

TdW 2005: *Typologie der Wünsche 2004/2005*. Erding: Institut für Medien- und Konsumentenforschung.

Wann, D.L. 2001: *Sport Fans: The Psychology and Social Impact of Spectators*. New York: Routledge.

Wicker, P., K. Hallmann, J. Prinz & D. Weimar 2012: Who Takes Part in Triathlon? An Application of Lifestyle Segmentation to Triathlon Participants. *International Journal of Sport Management and Marketing* 12:1/2, 1–24.

Wicker, P., J. Prinz & D. Weimar 2013: Big Spenders in a Booming Sport: Consumption Capital as a Key Driver of Triathletes' Sport-Related Expenditure. *Managing Leisure* (Online First Content).

Winkler, J. & K. Weis (eds.) 1995: *Soziologie des Sports: Theorieansätze, Forschungsergebnisse und Forschungsperspektiven*. Opladen: Westdeutscher Verlag.

Woodland, L. 2005: *This Island Race: Inside 135 Years of British Bike-Racing*. Norwich: Mousehold Press.

Stefan Groth is a post-doctoral fellow at the Käte Hamburger Kolleg/Centre for Global Cooperation Research, University Duisburg-Essen. As member of the Göttingen research unit on cultural property he has published "Negotiating Tradition: The Pragmatics of International Deliberations on Cultural Property" (Göttingen 2012). His research interests include cultural heritage, the relation between culture and cooperation, morality and cultural aspects of recreational sports. (sgroth@gwdg.de)

BILLIARDS, RHYTHMS, COLLECTIVES
Billiards at a Danish Activity Centre as a Culturally Specific Form of Active Ageing

Aske Juul Lassen

Building on an ethnographic study of older men playing billiards at an activity centre as well as document analysis of how the concept of activity has changed during the last sixty years, this article argues that active ageing policies have overlooked that activities are culturally significant forms of practice situated in socio-material collectives. Active ageing policies create a hierarchy amongst activities, wherein constant physical activity is at the core of a healthy old age. But in billiards, activity and passivity are meticulously composed into a rhythm that enables the players to engage for hours and that thus produces a collective practice. The article concludes that activity and passivity are entangled, and a game such as billiards contains qualities that could be translated into a revised active ageing policy.

Keywords: active ageing, everyday practices, older people, activity-passivity entanglement, culturally significant activities

Studying Active Ageing at The Cordial Club

The active ageing discourse forms current European ageing policies. Rather than portraying old age as a life stage of passiveness and decline, the active ageing discourse transforms late life into a period of physical activities and opportunities. But at activity centres in Denmark, different forms of active ageing appear than in the European Union (EU) and the World Health Organization (WHO) policy papers. This article[1] is about how older men playing billiards at the activity centre The Cordial Club challenge some of the configurations of late life inscribed into active ageing and how their practices suggest a different ideal of activity. Their practice raises questions about the ways in which active ageing is promoted, the kind of activities active ageing promotes (physical, social, mental, etc.) and how cultural difference engenders different kinds of activities that do not necessarily fit into the discourse of active ageing.

In Denmark, there are various kinds of activity centres for the retired. The centres have different characteristics depending on the types of activities they offer. Often, billiards is one of the most popular activities at the activity centres, and The Cordial Club in the capital area of Denmark is no exception. Almost all of the 110 active members participate in the club's billiards tournament. While billiards is often the most popular activity at activity centres, it is also associated with the pubs of industrial society's working class. The game seems somehow anachronistic and out of sync with the increasing focus on physical activity and self-care. At The Cordial Club, most members have a working-class background and have played billiards throughout their life course. Their life histories and traditions are amalgamated into the game and the table's green cloth. In this way, billiards is a culturally specific form of practice.

I have studied how the active ageing policy and discourse unfolds in practice through ethnographic fieldwork at The Cordial Club. From January 2011 to May 2013, I spent approximately 13 weeks doing participant observations at The Cordial Club. Furthermore, I conducted nine semi-structured interviews, each ranging from one to four hours, with some of the centre's members. I also followed three of the interviewees in their everyday activities, such as buying groceries, picking up grandchildren and participating in birthday parties and informal dinners. These everyday activities served as opportunities to observe different kinds of activities in a variety of settings.

The EU and the WHO have positioned active ageing as the solution to the demographic and economic challenges presented by the ageing European population (Zaidi et al. 2013; WHO 1999, 2008). Active ageing is a gerontologically-inspired political concept that aims to produce a more active late life for the elderly through a re-organisation of individual behaviour and societal structures (Lassen & Moreira 2014; Moulaert & Paris 2013; Boudiny 2013; Walker 2002). In particular, active ageing emphasises physical activity, social participation and a longer working life as central elements when it comes to improving the quality of life of older individuals as well as the economy (Stenner, McFarquhar & Bowling 2011). In this article, I regard active ageing as more than a policy tool and a gerontologically-inspired concept. It is also a discourse that produces ideals of the good late life; it is embedded in practice and forms differences and hierarchies amongst activities. With active ageing policies in mind, billiards is problematised as a physically passive activity. The older people's billiards game is politicised because of the type of activity it lacks: physical activity conducted in order to lead a healthy and long life. The collective at The Cordial Club does not promote a healthy lifestyle according to the active ageing discourse, but rather emphasises cordiality and togetherness.

As part of active ageing policy, a range of national pension reforms and local initiatives have been launched to change retirement behaviour, encourage more people to lead healthy and active lives into old age, and delay older people's dependence and need for care (EU 2012, 2011; WHO 2002). In Denmark, one of the local initiatives is the on-going development of activity centres like The Cordial Club. The centres are run by members and supported by the municipalities to varying degrees, and they offer facilities for – and/or instruction in – a range of activities during the week. These activities often focus on physical movement, such as Pilates, qigong, ping-pong, Zumba and gymnastics. However, the centres also offer different types of activities that are more focused on togetherness and conversation, such as billiards, knitting, stamp-collecting, and language classes, that is, activities that do not have physical fitness as the primary outcome.

The wide range of activities on offer suggests a comprehensive approach to active ageing. Indeed, as one of the slogans states, active ageing is both about "adding years to life and life to years" (European Senior Citizens Union 2003; WHO 2013). As global populations experience a radical growth in life expectancy (Christensen et al. 2009), it is crucial for healthcare systems and quality of life that individuals are free of disease during the extra years. Furthermore, as the slogan indicates, adding life to years also points to active ageing as more than a purely medical definition of health as absence of disease. The EU promotes a longer working life, but with regards to the post-retirement period, active ageing policy papers use a comprehensive terminology to describe the content of the extra years, including concepts such as "participation", "social inclusion" and "independence" (EC 2011).

However, in national adaptations and local initiatives, active ageing is often condensed into the promotion of physical activity, which is considered to be central to maintaining a healthy and active old age, according to the Danish Health and Medicines Authority (Sundhedsstyrelsen 2011). This complexity and contradiction between international policy apparatuses and their enactments in local practice has previously been the subject of ethnological studies concerned with the localisation of international conventions (Bendix, Eggert & Peselmann 2012) and Europeanisation as heterogeneous processes (Welz 2012; Sandberg 2009). While the condensation of active ageing policy into physical activity shows how Europeanisation is transformed in specific localities, it also reveals a hierarchy amongst different kinds of activities. Activities that offer cardiovascular exercise are valued higher than other types of activities. Whereas social activities were previously regarded as the most important type of activities and physical activities were regarded as dangerous for the old,

physical activities are now thought to be integral to a healthy old age. An increasing scientific consensus that physical activity is the single most important factor for health (WHO 1996) enforces this emphasis on physical activity. Physical activity has become the main activity that other types of activity can flourish around.

Although billiards is a physically strenuous exercise for some of the men at The Cordial Club, who play billiards five to six hours a day in old age, they do not focus on the strenuous aspect of billiards. To them, physical activity is an added benefit; they focus more on the social aspects of the activity. As I argue in the analysis, the emphasis on constant physical activity creates blindness towards these types of activities. The active ageing discourse produces an ideal type of late life focused on health, activity and

Ill. 1: The billiards room in The Cordial Club where the elderly men play billiards four days weekly. (Photo: Aske Juul Lassen 2011)

independence, in which constant physical activity is essential.

Stephen Katz has described the focus on activities for the elderly as part of a disciplinary management of post-retirement everyday life that creates independent "busy bodies" with less need for welfare support (2000). As suggested by David Ekerdt, there is a moral demand that the elderly remain busy (Ekerdt 1986). This "busy ethic" is a continuation of the work ethic into retirement. Retirees can use this to justify their leisure activities in retirement, and to defend themselves against being deemed obsolete. As long as their activities have a physical or productive aspect, then the specifics of what the retirees are busy with – that is, the content of the activities they engage in – are secondary to the fact that they remain busy. This establishes a certain hierarchy amongst post-retirement activities, in which physical activity is at the core of active ageing. In order to practise a normatively good type of ageing, the individual must engage in physical activity.

However, as shown in the analysis, for the players at The Cordial Club, the content of their activity is not secondary. To them, it is not about being active for the sake of activity and busy-ness itself. They cannot simply replace billiards with a more physically active type of activity. Billiards is an important and unifying aspect of their collective, as billiards materialises their life histories, family traditions, class affiliations and produces a particular rhythm in their everyday lives. However, the active ageing discourse disregards the cultural significance of billiards. The game of billiards illuminates some potential problems with the way the active ageing policies are configured locally: They must adapt to the rhythms of the everyday lives of older people, to the history and kind of collective in which they wish to intervene as well as to the cultural significance of the activities they try to promote. In order to do so, it is necessary to conduct ethnological analyses of older peoples' everyday practices, and the cultural and socio-material specificities in which active ageing is embedded.

I start out by presenting a brief overview of the concept of activity in social gerontology. I demonstrate how the focus on the older individual has its roots in the emphasis on individual adjustment through activity in post-World War II social gerontology. I also illustrate how the anachronistic status of the billiards table is a consequence of changes to the concept of activity during the last fifty years. Furthermore, I describe how cultural gerontologists have previously criticised active ageing. I then present the theoretical framework of the article and show how I use actor-network theory (ANT) to focus on the collective rhythms in The Cordial Club, and to overcome the dichotomy between activity and passivity. Before turning to my empirical analysis, I describe how I have used billiards as the "kitchen entrance" (Ehn & Löfgren 2006) to active ageing, and how this analytical strategy has also been a methodological choice that has allowed me to use my difference from the interviewees and my inability to play billiards – my out-of-sync-ness – as a "productive disturbance".

The Concept of Activity in Active Ageing and Social Gerontology

The concept of activity has been central to social gerontology since the birth of the discipline in the late 1940s (Cavan 1949; Pollak 1948). In the middle of the twentieth century – a time when pension reforms and compulsory retirement shaped "old age" as a new distinct period of life – activities were a way to organise schedules and older people's everyday lives through the theoretical framework of activity theory, which highlighted the importance of activity to individual well-being in old age (Katz 2000). However, the concept of "activity" has profoundly changed from 1950 to 2014; specifically, the emphasis has shifted from the social to the physical.

In the 1950s, compulsory retirement was still new in most countries worldwide. The burgeoning discipline of social gerontology examined what happens to an older individual when he or she is released from the constraints and commitments of work and family (Havighurst 1969). At the time, the social sciences were strongly influenced by the functionalistic currents from Talcott Parsons (1902–1979) and Émile Durkheim (1858–1917), who emphasised the totality of society and the importance of individuals serving a specific function within this totality. An individual's well-being was closely linked to the assignment of a social role, which changed with retirement. The individual needed to adjust to a new social role that was inferior to that of the working individual (Cavan 1949).

After retirement, activities were expected to compensate for the social relationships left behind at the workplace, and the elderly were expected to engage in new age-appropriate activities (Havighurst 1954). Social gerontology engaged in listing these activities, which ranged from taking care of grandchildren to playing bingo, billiards, cards and other games. These activities were meant to facilitate a new type of social life and should ideally be supplemented with an increased involvement in the church (Cavan 1949). In gerontological literature from that period, physical activity is rarely mentioned; when it is, the emphasis is on light physical activities appropriate for the age group, such as square-dancing or playing billiards and shuffleboard (Michelon 1954; Pressey & Simcoe 1950; Zahrobsky 1950). Billiards was suitable as a social activity for the elderly, as it only involves mild physical exertion and encourages conversation and togetherness.

By the 2000s, the range of appropriate activities for the elderly had become radically different. Social activities are still considered to be important, but the emphasis now is on physical and productive activity (Walker 2006; WHO 1998). Whereas the mild physical activity involved in playing billiards was an asset in the 1950s, it is now a detriment. This change has occurred due to a process of scientification and medicalisation of old age. The relationship between health and physical activity was only firmly established during the second half of the twentieth century (WHO 1996). Earlier medical studies did not focus on the possible benefits of physical activity for health and longevity. Instead, they sought to measure whether physical activity was dangerous and could cause strokes. This changed in the 1960s when studies showed a possible relationship between health and physical activity (e.g., Schnohr 1968). Physical activity as the key to remaining healthy throughout life has only been a scientific fact since the late twentieth century, and was not extensively promoted prior to that.

By the end of the 1980s, physical activity entered gerontology, due in part to Row and Kahn's work on "successful ageing" (Rowe & Kahn 1987). The concept emphasised the individual's influence on – and responsibility for – his or her own physiological ageing process. By the 1990s, senescence was becoming the result of an unhealthy individual lifestyle. This individualisation of the responsibility for a "good" ageing process also entailed what has been termed a "biomedicalisation of old age" (Estes & Binney 1989). Numerous studies showed that physical activity could prevent or delay multiple conditions – from cancer to dementia, as well as cardiovascular diseases, metabolic diseases, gout and arthritis. Physical activity is also believed to be beneficial for cognitive function (Angevaren et al. 2008), social relations and quality of life (WHO 1996). Physical activity was established as an integral part of health and successful ageing. As the components of what comprised an appropriate old age were transformed, billiards was deemed overly sedentary. It was part of a former ideal of old age.

The increased emphasis on physical activity has changed the typology of appropriate activities for the elderly. In the 1950s, strenuous physical activity was thought to be dangerous as it would put the elderly at risk of strokes and injuries, but now it is one of the most important factors in the "good life" of an older person (WHO 1998, 1999). And, to a certain extent, older people have adapted to this paradigm – studies show that more older persons are exercising (Pilgaard 2009). For an older person today, it is not only appropriate to engage in strenuous physical activity, the active ageing discourse includes a subtle demand for physical activity that will facilitate a long and healthy life. While this one-dimensional focus on physical activity might pave the road to a healthier old age, it risks overlooking that activities – physical and nonphysical – are culturally specific forms of practice.

Cultural gerontologists have argued that this emphasis on physical activity leaves little space for other types of (in)activities usually related to old age, such as napping (Venn & Arber 2011). In this way, constant activity is construed as the ideal, and inactivity is stigmatised as unproductive, sedentary and a negative sign of ageing. The healthy ageing process implies constant activity. In a British study of older peoples' images of other older people, inactive older people are portrayed as the *villains of old age* and passivity is described as part of an antiquated image of old age associated with grumpiness and giving up (Townsend, Godfrey & Denby 2006). This stigmatisation has led to concerns that the "new old age" overly idealises old age, ignores the decline and hardship that can also be a part of the ageing process, and inserts normative and oppressive standards that most older persons cannot live up to (Holstein & Minkler 2007; Katz 2001).

However, this does not mean that older persons are not active, but rather that their activities often have purposes other than health, longevity or productivity. What active ageing policies define as good activities is different to the point of view of the elderly, who might perceive planning for death, entering residential care, or ordinary needs and deeds as good activities (Clarke & Warren 2007). Thus, there is a need for further research into the particularities of older peoples' practices and experiences (Holstein & Minkler 2007). An ethnological approach can illuminate these particularities. For example, the present study shows how the active ageing discourse unfolds in the particular Danish, working-class collective of The Cordial Club, and how insights that can be transported to other kinds of activities appear through this collective.

Theoretical Framework

The problematisation of active ageing policies and "the new old age" has often been based on either a critical gerontological point of view, inspired by the theory of structured dependency[2] (Townsend 1981), or on a Foucauldian governmentality approach (e.g., Biggs & Powell 2001; Katz 1996). Although these approaches have been fruitful, I suggest another theoretical framework for studying how active ageing is negotiated and unfolds in socio-material practices.

By applying ANT (Latour 1987) to ageing studies, I am able to focus on the collective socio-material practice of playing billiards, dissolve the dichotomy between activity and passivity often present in active ageing policy, and suggest how the rhythms of the game hint at a different version of active ageing, which builds upon existing, functioning and specific forms of activities.

One of the major contributions of ANT to ethnology has been a renewed emphasis on the materiality of cultural processes. While this renewal cannot solely be ascribed to ANT, it is part of a larger "material turn" in ethnology with several theoretical sources of inspiration (Damsholt & Simonsen 2009; Otto 2005). Bruno Latour has suggested that the distinction between humans and things is highly anthropocentric, and that agency is always deeply entangled in networks of human and non-human actors, which he designates "actants" (1988, 1991). This entanglement suggests that practices are socio-material rather than solely social. When the older people at The Cordial Club play billiards, they do so in a meticulously composed collective rhythm wherein the human and non-human actants make the game run as smoothly as possible – they seem to dance with each other.

Following the same line of thought, in his analysis of patient collectives, Tiago Moreira defines collectives as "compositions of bodies, competences, artefacts, procedures and emotions gathered together by particular activities" (Moreira 2004: 35). In this article, billiards is the particular activity that gathers the collective in a composition of bodies (players), competences (billiards skills, tricks, social competences), artefacts (the table, beers, equipment), procedures (rhythms of the game) and emotions (life histories, class affiliations).

Whereas the older person is constantly urged to be active in the present active ageing discourse, there are different rhythms within the billiards game. This allows for moments of passivity, which is important for the players in their old age. In their article about drug users and music lovers, Emilie Gomart and Antoine Hennion suggest that it is a misunderstanding to construe activity–passivity as a dichotomy: rather, the states of activity and passivity constitute each other – they are entangled. In order to be passively immersed in music, music-lovers have to actively arrange the passive immersion through socio-material practices, in order to create the perfect environment and sound system (1999). In the same way, billiards is composed of both activity and passivity, and allows for a rhythmic movement between the two. Billiards is both activity and passivity, and the separation of the two attenuates the active ageing policies by promoting constant activity.

Analytical Strategy and Methodology

The analytical strategy in this article resembles what Billy Ehn and Orvar Löfgren have termed "the kitchen entrance" of culture (2006). By paying attention to the seemingly insignificant trivialities of everyday life, such as morning routines, the cultural analyst can study how such everyday practises are entangled with larger cultural processes. In this regard, billiards is a specific and collective form of cultural practice that points to the way activities are usually limited to physical activities in the active ageing discourse. Billiards challenges the active ageing discourse by demonstrating the normative and individualistic aspects of the focus on physical activity and a healthy lifestyle. To play billiards is to be active, but in a different manner than suggested by the present active ageing discourse.

Participant observations at the activity centre allowed me to focus on the specific practice of playing billiards, and also served as a way to meet interview subjects. The interviews were conducted at the interviewees' homes in order to gain a differently situated understanding of their practice. Although I also engaged with the interviewees at the centre during participant observations, the nine semi-structured interviews provided different accounts of the everyday lives of the interviewees and insights about the different relations and networks that formed their practice. The different fieldwork settings contributed to the production of diverse fieldwork materials (notes, photos, recordings and collection of objects from the field) and allowed me to include second opinions about the interviewees' practices from their wives, children, grandchildren and friends from outside the activity centre, as well as from the various situations and accounts that the change of setting created. The details of billiards and active ageing were accentuated in different ways and gained ethnographic richness thanks to the diversity of sites and material produced.

I consider active ageing to be a policy concept and a discourse, and I follow it through its multi-sited configurations and enactments in everyday practices. This also means that I am an integral part of performing the field through my understanding of active ageing, which I have achieved by reading literature and documents, via participant observations, and through my analysis that relates active ageing and billiards. The field is performed through the collective practices, my reading of them, and the interplay between these phenomena (Coleman & Collins 2006; cf. Jespersen 2007).

Using Ehn and Löfgren's (2006) line of thinking, billiards may be understood as the "kitchen entrance" of active ageing, as it shows how active ageing can unfold in practice, and how it is negotiated in this practice. However, as I entered through the kitchen door of active ageing, the structure and decoration of this kitchen were changed. The game of billiards was disturbed by my presence. My age and background differed from the old working-class men at the activity centre and my skills as a billiards player differed from the Cordial Club's billiards players. The rhythm, order and smoothness of the game were thus severely compromised by my lack of skills, as well as my lack of understanding of the small gestures and things that make up the game. I thus realised how "out of sync" I was with the game. While this positioned me as an outsider, it also allowed me to consider what it was that I disturbed – and it inspired me to see the routines in their absence, and the rhythm through its disruption. In this way, my out-of-sync-ness became a methodological and analytical strategy, and a condition for what I was able to observe. My presence interrupted the game and revealed how its cultural specificity makes it fragile for intruders, but simultaneously makes it durable through its many practices, actants and intertwinements with the participants' life histories.

In the following empirical sections, I examine billiards as a socio-material practice that is embedded in a specific type of "good late life", which nuances the "good late life" currently promoted in EU and WHO active ageing policies. By showing the cultural significance of billiards, I demonstrate how active ageing risks producing specific and confined configurations of individuals and collectives that are ignorant to cultural practices, and that exclude alternative functioning collectives. As described by Jespersen and colleagues, one of the ambitions of cultural analysis should be to engage in the composition of "common worlds" (2012). Perhaps playing billiards could be re-composed – not as a common activity for all older persons – but as a specific form of active ageing activity that promotes social participation and engagement in life, with physical activity as an added benefit.

The Cordial Club – an Active Ageing Collective

Wagner leans over to shoot the ball. From the way he slowly and stiffly leans over, it is obvious that he has spent a long life carrying around sacks of potatoes as a greengrocer. At 91 years of age, he is one of the oldest players at the club. Wagner shoots the ball slowly and with control – with precision and the right pace. He has had his cue stick for many years, and began playing as a kid in the 1930s. He and his fellow players often play billiards from 10.00 to 16.00, three to four times a week.

As Wagner maintains his bent-over position, his eyes follow his slow and controlled shot. His back is stiff, but he is still able to control his shots – most of the time, at least. He complains that he is beginning to lose more games, and he is disappointed in many of his shots. What looks like a masterful shot – the perfect alignment between Wagner, cue stick, ball and table – turns out to be misleading. One does not have to see the balls roll to know that the shot is bad; it is visible in Wagner's eyes. He stands up straight, steps back into a passive state and waits for his next turn. Sometimes, he talks a bit with his fellow players, but mostly he waits and helps replace the pins after the ball has hit them.[3] He is primarily passive between turns. He focuses on the game, looks at the details, and watches how the balls roll on the green table. And just when I think he has lost focus, it is his turn again, and he immediately walks around the table. With a lifetime of experience, he has the ability to know exactly the right place from which to make his shot. He leans over...

The member-driven Cordial Club is located in an activity centre for the elderly in a suburban municipality on the outskirts of Copenhagen. Founded in the 1950s as "Billardklubben" (The Billiards Club), it was originally a self-organised billiards club for a group of blue-collar, male workers at an electronics factory, which had billiards facilities. In the 1980s, when the members were reaching retirement age, they wanted to continue their billiards club and had no place to go. They discovered that if they became an official association, they could use the public facilities at the newly opened municipal activity centre next to the factory. Many of the members' wives were also retiring and needed a place to meet and socialise, sew or play cards and dice. Thus, because a "billiards club was no place for a lady" (as a female member, Tove, said during my participant observations), Billardklubben changed its name to The Cordial Club and became an open association for all retirees in the municipality.

The Cordial Club is located in the bar and café areas of an activity centre. All members are retirees and the majority of members are older than 70 years of age. Most members are in their 70s and 80s and a few are in their 90s. The Cordial Club is member-driven and has its own board with a chairman, treasurer and several committees for parties, excursions, etc. There are 30 to 40 core members who run the club and attend three to four times a week. The rest of the members only occasionally come by for the bi-weekly bingo games or to attend parties and excursions. The most frequent users are the men who play billiards, but there are also 10 to 15 women who come three to four times a week to play dice, cards, darts, and to make lunch.

Ironically, the activity centre is now located in the former buildings of the now-defunct electronics factory. Although most of the club's current members did not work at the factory, many of them share a working-class background, and they often say that this is one of the things that make them feel at home at the club. Their shared background distinguishes The Cordial Club from other types of activity centres. The members used to work on the same factory floors, and many of their routines, jargon and the way they see themselves – in opposition to policy, municipality, health and physical activity – creates a kind of alignment among the members.

There is no doubt that other forms of activity for the elderly, with a more specific focus on physical activity, would suit the active ageing discourse better. However, billiards is a popular activity in which many older persons participate, and, when entered from the "kitchen door", it can be seen as a form of active ageing since it activates the elderly, allows them to take part, engage socially, and form their own type of collective. In many respects, it fits well with the overall guidelines of active ageing policy. However, the aspects of the game that do not fit in are the ones that stand out: the working-class jargon, alcohol consumption and indifference towards health guidelines and physical activity.

Although The Cordial Club and the billiards game have an anachronistic feeling of "out-of-sync-ness" attached to them, they are at the centre of active ageing policy. Municipalities and the EU support activity centres. Activity centres configure activities as the structuring principle of post-retirement everyday life, and create the framework within which older persons can organise themselves around activities. In this way, activity centres are policy tools that produce certain types of active late lives. While the older men in The Cordial Club might differ from the ideal active ageing subject, there are many of their kind in Denmark; collectives of older men who do not engage in activities because they are supposed to be healthy, but because they ascribe certain values and histories to the type of activities they engage in, and because they enjoy the social togetherness and friendship surrounding the activity.

The activities at "The Cordial Club" are not specifically physical activities. However, playing billiards five to six hours a day is a physical achievement for many of the members. In this way, billiards is a physical activity, but it is not articulated as such by the members. There is not much talk about health at the club, and the members often consider leaving the house to be an achievement in and of itself, at their age. When they do talk about health, they often ironically talk about "the health regime", and how their doctors worry more about their health than they do. Many members talk about physical ailments as an intrinsic part of reaching their age, and they think the doctors should just let them enjoy themselves instead of making them feel guilty about their "unhealthy" lifestyles. Alcohol consumption is an integrated part of the collective, and it is considered to be something their doctors should not interfere with. Hence, the members do not openly adhere to the active ageing discourse, although the ideals of activity and health are often used as implicit standards when they talk about their diets, gardening work, winter-bathing or gymnastics (for an elaboration of this point see Lassen 2014). In this way, the members ambiguously inscribe many of their activities into a health-oriented active ageing discourse.

Billiards as Affiliation, Tradition and Escape

My dad used to take me to the pub and teach me how to play. (…) When there were birthdays, all of the men would go out to play as soon as dinner was over. I remember the first time I was old enough to go, 10 or 11 years old, a big day. (Kaare)[4]

For Kaare, 80 years of age, billiards is not just amusement – it is part of his family history; billiards has been passed down from generation to generation, and entering the male collective of billiards players was part of becoming a man. When Kaare was young in the 1940s and 1950s, playing billiards was a way to socialise, but also a place for education and passing on traditions. The younger generations were taken to the pub when they were old enough to learn how to play, and to learn how to be part of a working-class collective. The adults taught the adolescents how to socialise and work; playing billiards was a way to prepare them for the jargon at the factory floor. Kaare remembers the first time his father took him to the pub to play:

I remember the smell of beer and tobacco, the low lights inside the pub – everything as you'd expect it to be, probably. My father's brothers and friends all showed me what to do and were very welcoming. I felt like a man sometimes, but at the next moment, they would tease me about a bad shot or some kind of awkwardness, and I would become very little again. (...) This was a new world opening up to me – some skill that I had to acquire, and I wanted to – needed to, really. When my father gave me my first cue stick, I knew that I was part of it. They had taught me how to play and how to behave like a man. (Kaare)

In Kaare's family, there was a transfer of skills and knowledge from generation to generation. But now, the younger generations in Kaare's family resist receiving the skills and knowledge to play billiards. At family birthday parties, the men still go out to play after dinner, but the younger generation appears disinterested when they are at the pub. Kaare sees this as a loss of tradition.

Karl, 79 years of age, also considers billiards to be a part of his family history. He comes from a family of billiards-table carpenters. One of his uncles worked for a famous billiards-table manufacturer and, as a teenager, Karl worked as an assistant, along with his friend and future brother-in-law. The brother-in-law continued to work as a billiards-table carpenter – a fact in which Karl takes great pride. More than half a century ago, Karl himself assembled one of the still-standing billiards tables at The Cordial Club, and he constantly judges the (lack of) skills and effort put into the maintenance of the tables by the service personnel of the billiards-table company:

It's a craftsmanship that has disappeared. When I was young, we took pride in our skills with the tables. It was a matter of accuracy and detail and skill. And we played ourselves, you see, everyone in my family. Now, they don't know what they're doing. You can sense it when you're playing on the table. I always have to fix it after [they've fixed it], but [I have] no tools anymore, so sometimes we call them again. I wish my brother-in-law hadn't retired. It's a craftsmanship that has disappeared, really. (Karl)

At The Cordial Club, nostalgia is part of the billiards game. There is a lot of talk about the good old days on the factory floors and "friendly bullying", as they call it, when they make fun of each other using their working-class jargon, as well as sentimental accounts of the time when one was allowed to smoke and drink without being frowned upon. They have a special way of saying cheers without noisily clinking their bottles together. This small gesture is a way to show class affiliation, as they said cheers in this way at the different factories where they worked, so that the factory manager would not hear them drinking alcohol before lunch.

For most of the players at The Cordial Club, billiards has been a leisure activity throughout their lives. However, it has changed over time: many of the players describe how billiards has become a strenuous activity. Previously, it was just a social activity, but when one is 80 or 90 years of age and plays billiards five to six hours a day, it is a physically demanding activity, and one's body aches afterwards. Wagner, 91 years of age, describes it as such:

I didn't understand it at first when I started coming here. I was sore in the mornings and felt like I did when I was an apprentice bricklayer back in the day. Then it hit me. I wasn't used to playing billiards for so many hours anymore. You know you're an old geezer when your body hurts after playing billiards. (Wagner)

For Wagner the continuity and duration of the billiards game and the rhythm of playing for so many hours is an achievement. While active ageing's emphasis on physical activity and health has turned billiards into a sedentary type of activity, it has simultaneously become a tougher physical activity for these elderly people as they get older and still play for hours on end. In this way, the players inscribe billiards into an activity ideal:

It might not be marathon running, but at my age and with my health, this is an achievement. I don't sit at home on the couch. So what if I have a couple of beers? I'm here, out the house, talking to the guys, walking around, playing. That's what counts, isn't it? To do something, to enjoy life. (Bent, during a game of billiards)

In this quote Bent, 78 years of age, relates the state of doing "something" to enjoying life. For him, an important aspect of billiards is that it is comprised of both social and physical activity. In the terminology of social gerontology from the 1940s, billiards is a form of adjustment (Cavan 1949; Pollak 1948). However, what one must adjust to has changed. Bent emphasises not just the social aspect but also the physical, although he is not generally concerned with his health. He and his fellow players inscribe billiards into the "busy ethic" (Ekerdt 1986); they need to be active and busy in order to enjoy life.

Billiards can bring together the collective through the emotions it awakens in the players, and via its intertwinement with their life histories. Several of the players told me an almost identical story about how they searched for something meaningful to do and a suitable place to go after they retired. Through different channels, they heard about the billiards tables at The Cordial Club, visited the place and immediately felt at home. Billiards is an important aspect of this feeling-at-home; it carries the history of the players' lives. The feeling of belonging is not just produced by the game or the tables but rather by the entire collective and the history of which it is a part:

The social workers told me about the place. They saw that I was exhausted from taking care of my wife [who was suffering from dementia] and arranged for her to go to a day-care centre twice a week so I could go to the club. When I walked in, I recognised a lot of the members. Some had been customers at my shop, some were from my neighbourhood, others I had played with at the local pubs. This is a nice place, you know. We look out for each other, tease each other, help each other, and cheat each other, but always with a gleam in our eyes. This place, the beers, the beautiful tables, the guys, the lunches, the games and the atmosphere – it instantly made my shoulders drop a couple of centimetres. I was stressed out, but this place changed that. I asked [when entering the first time] what it would take for me to play with them. The bastards told me to buy a round of beers, and I did. When I found out afterwards from Kirstine [the chairman at the time] that I just had to become a member to play, and the round of beers was something they made up, my shoulders dropped a couple of centimetres more. (Wagner)

Wagner immediately felt at home at The Cordial Club. His shared history of drinking and playing billiards at the local pubs with several of the other players confirmed that this was the type of collective in which he would like to engage during his retirement. At The Cordial Club, he could continue to show off and develop the billiards skills he had honed and performed his entire life. Many of the players at The Cordial Club have severe problems with their health and struggle with loneliness, but billiards creates a refuge where these issues are forgotten. The interviewees Stig and Valter consider billiards and The Cordial Club to be a temporary escape from the loneliness they feel at home, and Karl frequents the billiards tables more often now that his wife suffers from depression, as he needs a break from the atmosphere at home.

When the players talk about physical activity, it is usually with reference to the "health regime". In this collective, diseases and decline are intrinsic parts of growing older. Some say that their doctors worry more than they do about their risk of developing high blood pressure, high cholesterol, type 2 diabetes and arthritis. Some of the members even articulate that cardiovascular diseases and heart surgery are just a part of getting old and not something that should get in the way of a good game of billiards for very long, nor make one worry excessively. When I asked Bent, who was sitting in a chair watching the others play if he was playing that day, he responded:

No. They've just given me a new "thingamajig"[5], you see. The heart didn't work anymore so they had to fix the apparatus and change the "thingamajig" there [pointing to his chest]. So they said I had to relax a bit, and it hurts when I move my left arm, so I can't play billiards. But luckily, there's nothing wrong with my right arm [he laughs as he uses his right hand to take a sip of beer]. (Bent, while watching a game of billiards)

Billiards is a huge part of Bent's life. He comes to The Cordial Club to watch the games and be part of the collective, even though he cannot play. But he is still able to participate in the conversations, drink beer and immerse himself in the other players' games. He has recently undergone a serious surgery, but he seems more concerned about his current inability to play billiards than his health. In his case, health is directly related to his ability to play billiards: "I'm ill if I can no longer play billiards" (Bent, while watching a game of billiards). Thus, Bent links his health to his capacity to play billiards, and it is one of the central activities of daily living that he wants to regain the ability to perform.

The specific configuration of the collective at The Cordial Club produces the "good late life" as one in which togetherness, class affiliation, billiards, beer, mild physical activity, leaving the house, a cosy atmosphere and participation are all part of the composition. In this way, it is not an outright rejection of active ageing; rather, it transforms active ageing and inserts it into a culturally specific practice.

A Game Composed of Activity and Passivity

When Wagner plays billiards he is in a state that is neither passive nor active. While he is active for many hours – he walks around, stands up, replaces the pins, leans over, shoots, etc. – he also spends a lot of his time at the activity centre passively immersed in the game; he gets into its rhythm. This rhythm sometimes entails longer periods of passivity, as there are usually too many players for the centre's three tables. While an excess of players could pose a problem, it allows them to play for a longer period of time as it forces one or two players to take breaks while the others play. During these breaks, the players waiting often have a conversation or comment on the shots being made. But usually, the players use their breaks to drink a beer and stare at the game; to get immersed in it. The states of passivity and activity are entangled and part of the same practice. There is continuity between them: activity is not just activity, and passivity is not just passivity. They are entangled.

The dance between activity and passivity is meticulously composed and refined over many years of playing. I constantly place myself in the wrong position and do little things too fast or at the wrong moment. The older players play calmly. They know where to position themselves so they are not in the way of the player shooting or the one keeping score. They tacitly perform the various tasks between them. They know when to place the pins, when to take a sip of beer, when and where to be passive, who is buying the next round of beers and when to converse. Although they are very welcoming to outsiders, it is hard not to feel out of place. They do not seem to acknowledge that I am out of sync; instead, they smile and explain the rules of the game when I ask. But I am out of place, and when I occasionally lead the scoreboard in the beginning of a game, they notice and comment on the humorous aspect of it. Then it becomes clear that I am not really in sync, not part of their collective. When my participation is not interfering in their game, they appear to dance without thinking about it. My presence disturbs the collective.

Despite their advanced age, the players appear to effortlessly enter the rhythm of the game. They weave around each other and gracefully hit the balls with just the right force. My approach to billiards is more arbitrary, and I ruin some of the grace of their game. Sometimes, I shoot too hard. At other times, I estimate that my best chance for success is a hard shot that will make the white balls bounce back and forth and eventually hit the pins. But this assessment is usually wrong, and my wild shots end up giving the other players points that are decisive for many of the games I participate in.

My participation adds an element of chaos to an

otherwise smooth composition. However, the older players do not seem to be frustrated by this – over a lifetime of playing billiards, they have played with chaotic players many times and know how to slowly teach new players to adapt to the rhythm – but they do notice the chaos. Karl previously told me that playing with the women, and some of the guys, was not fun. I soon learned what he was talking about, and that he was also talking about me. It is not these players' lack of competitiveness or their inability to correctly keep score; rather, it is the fact that the game becomes more arbitrary and less rhythmic. Chaotic players often create advantageous positions for the following players and their wild shots may be decisive for a game. Furthermore, doubts about who is going to do what arise. The rhythm is disrupted, and the players cannot show the same level of attentiveness towards the game. Here, billiards is not about winning but about playing the game, becoming immersed in the game, continuing the game and honouring the game by making the right shot and devoting one's full attention to the game.

"You almost did a Bent", teases Kaare, after Johnny shoots with such force that the balls randomly bounce back and forth across the table. Johnny does not score, but he does come close. Bent is "one of the guys" and highly respected by the others, but he is also infamous for his chaotic style of play that involves many coincidences. He shoots with great force and racks up a lot of points that way, but the other players also earn many points from his chaotic shots. "You almost did a Bent" is a reference to Bent's chaotic and typically lucky shots. But Johnny does not take the teasing to heart, as he knows that the others recognise his usually controlled way of playing and know that his chaotic shot was a mistake.

The entire composition of the game is characterised by control and respect for the game. The players, beers, cue sticks, balls, pins, the table's green cloth and the scoreboard are all in perfect balance. They have played here together for many years and have composed a specific rhythm of play in which chaos and chance are disregarded. However, a player may be forced to shoot forcefully if there are no other alternatives. This is considered risky, but is also widely acclaimed when it scores points. The players notice when a shot is too hard, and most of the shots are slow and fully in control. A shot that is less forceful is more appreciated, as a soft tap honours the gracefulness of the game. A soft shot shows the others that the shooting player has understood the logic and complexity of the game, even if the shot is unsuccessful.

However, this controlled and meticulously composed dance also involves different rhythms – some of which upset the delicate balance between activity and passivity. As I describe in the next section, the different rhythms emphasise how billiards produces a specific type of "good late life" that balances activity and passivity. Some of the players trick each other and go to great lengths to maintain this equilibrium, avoiding rhythms of the game that provide less opportunity for passivity.

Rhythms, Tricks and Collectives

Prior to the first game of the day, the players usually take a shot to decide who will keep score; the player with the worst shot must keep score. After the first game, this task then meanders among the players, who take turns keeping score with the exception of the most disabled players. However, the designated scorekeeper often tries to fool the others into thinking it is someone else's turn. Attempting to avoid keeping score is part of the dance. If the player is not prepared for this, the others will make him believe it is his turn to keep score. And once the player has started to keep score, he is stuck doing it for the rest of that game.

The task of keeping score is disliked because it requires a different, constantly active, rhythm for the game. The scorekeeper cannot be passive between turns, but must constantly go back and forth between the table and the scoreboard. The other players will often try to trick him with the scores – for example, when he does not see a shot because he is busy tallying the score after the previous shot. Keeping score demands constant activity, constant calculations, constant movement of the markers on the scoreboard and a constant awareness of the shots. And then it is the scorekeeper's turn to play. Thus, the same game has several rhythms.

The delegation of tasks seems automatic most of the time – that is, until somebody tries to trick one of the other players. Then the game's rhythms become negotiable. Becoming immersed in the game without the hassle of keeping score is the ideal, as it allows for the movement between passivity and activity. Some players make up stories and use different tricks to avoid keeping score. However, they jokingly and smilingly accept their turn at keeping score if the others see through their tricks. The players accept the tricks as part of their collective game, and as part of their way of playing billiards. The collective forms itself as a group that has its own set of rules, and does not confine itself to what might be considered correct. To take turns, to be healthy and to be physically active are qualities in contrast to how the collective forms itself as an inclusive and alternative ageing collective. The tricks and cheating are part of the collective.

The collective has its own jargon. Some of the tricks used to avoid keeping score are so cleverly or remarkably designed and performed that they are named after the person who invented them. As already mentioned in relation to Bent, this is also the case with certain special shots that some of the players make, either due to a particular playing style or because a physical disability forces a player to shoot in a certain way when the ball is in a difficult position. Naming the shots and tricks is a procedure that forms The Cordial Club as a collective with its own terminology and jargon, which are occasionally incomprehensible to an outsider.

Just as the games have many rhythms, many tricks, and many shifting players, there are also many entities that compose the game. In addition to the human entities – such as the players and their (dis)abilities, the craftsmen who made the billiards table, the board members of The Cordial Club, the municipal officials, etc. – non-human entities also compose the collective: the green table, the cue sticks, the balls, the pins, the chairs, the beers, the scoreboard, etc. These artefacts are part of the collective and part of the production of procedures, such as the rhythm of the game, the ways of drinking, the entanglement between activity and passiv-ity, etc. These artefacts produce billiards as a socio-material practice.

In the collective, the social and the material are indistinguishable and entangled. Billiards is composed not only by the player keeping score, but also by how the scoreboard allows this player to keep score with a pin going from 0 to 100, as well as by how these numbers determine the shooting player's strategy. Billiards is composed not only by the way the players say cheers without clinking their beer bottles, but also by the sound the bottles would make if they did touch, and by the shared history of factory floors and the working-class background that this suggests. Billiards is composed not only by the way the players sit in their chairs between games, but also by the softness of the chairs and their placement, which allows for both conversation and silent immersion in the game.

Billiards produces a specific type of good late life and a certain way of ageing. The game's procedures, the conversations, the artefacts and the players produce a rhythm in the life of the players. They attend The Cordial Club, play billiards, eat lunch, talk with the other players, go home and repeat this rhythm the next day. It is not a type of active ageing that focuses on physical activity, health or productivity, but rather one that focuses on the collective, social activity and enjoying life in this specific manner. For the collective to work, the players have to look out for each other and require each other's attendance. Billiards composes the good late life as a life that is focused on togetherness and mutual care. This type of activity is a way to keep going rather than to exercise. But billiards does involve physical activity, due to the many hours of play each day. Thus, billiards could be inscribed into a different active ageing discourse that reorders the hierarchy of activities and focuses on the significance of the activity rather than on the outcomes of the activity – such as health or longevity.

Active ageing in The Cordial Club is not primarily about physical activity or health, nor is it an instrumental activity for the sake of activity itself. In this collective, billiards is not a random activity or a way to pass time that can be replaced by some other activity; instead, it is a culturally significant socio-material practice that links the players to their shared histories on the factory floors, and allows them to create their own procedures and rhythms. The socio-material practice creates room for an alternative form of active ageing that considers culturally significant everyday practices to be examples of what active ageing could become. This type of active ageing does not focus on physical activity, good health or productivity, nor does it discount the decline that often comes with late life. Rather, it embraces a form of late life that allows for limited physical abilities, different rhythms, different states of activity and passivity and culturally specific forms of practice. But it is not just billiards as it was 50 years ago. Billiards today is an active ageing activity because it produces subjects who are socially, physically and mentally active, and who are aware of – and emphasise the importance of – the activating aspects of playing billiards.

The case of billiards contains some insights that are transferable to other kinds of activities. Indeed, billiards is not the only type of activity at the activity centres that does not have physical activity and health as its primary outcome. Petanque, smithy workshops, knitting, darts, sewing, stone polishing, skittles, etc. all entail physical activity to some degree, but focus on other aspects of the activity; physical activity is an added benefit. In the same way, the rhythmic movement between activity and passivity can be seen in other activities. This is important not only for the participants' ability to engage in the activity for many hours, but also includes older people with various degrees of (dis)ability, composes a rhythm with space and time for breaks, beers and other endeavours, and thus knits the collective together. The type of collective described in this article shows how active ageing initiatives are situated in culturally specific localities. This collective calls for an ethnological approach that can scrutinise how everyday life unfolds and is entangled with larger cultural and political processes. Indeed, if the EU and WHO active ageing policies are to add life to years, and not just years to life, this approach is required in order to create active ageing policies that

recognise activities as cultural significant forms of practice. In this way I have attempted to re-compose active ageing and create a "common world" through cultural analysis.

Conclusion

Many current active ageing initiatives have a biomedical focus on physical activity and healthy lifestyle at their core. These types of initiatives aim to add more disease-free years to life, and this is seen as a pre-condition for a good old age. While the formulations of active ageing in the policy documents are very comprehensive and emphasise participation and engagement in life, these ambitions often disappear in the local active ageing initiatives. In its focus on physical activity and lifestyle, the biomedical approach produces a hierarchy amongst activities, wherein activities that have physical fitness as their outcome are more highly valued than activities that simply "keep you going". This creates blindness towards the cultural significance of the activities that unfold in the everyday practices at the activity centres.

Through an ethnological study of billiards at The Cordial Club, I have studied how the active ageing discourse is situated in a group of older men's collective socio-material practice. The older people I studied are very active, but in a different manner to that which is proposed by the EU and the WHO. The older people in this study do not particularly care about physical activity, nor are they concerned about health or want to work into very old age. The collective forms and negotiates what active ageing means via its practice. Active ageing in The Cordial Club is collective and composed of many bodies, artefacts, competences and procedures. Furthermore, it has cultural significance for the players due to their shared life histories – it is amalgamated into their lives. In this way it is a socio-material and cultural form of active ageing.

Although billiards is a specific form of practice rooted in a male, working-class, suburban collective, it includes some patterns that are transferable to other forms of activities and could become a guideline for how to translate active ageing policy into local initiatives. Through a coordinated distribution of tasks and gestures, the billiards collective forms a meticulously composed rhythm of activity and passivity. Activity and passivity are not opposites; they should be seen as states that are entangled and condition each other. This entanglement forms a durable collective that allows for players to play for many hours daily and includes frail people in very old ages. This is the local realisation of the active ageing ideal of independence and participation in old age. Nevertheless, this type of collective and activity seems out of sync with active ageing policies. Through its negotiation and transformation of active ageing, the billiards collective points to how active ageing can be anchored in the everyday life of the elderly.

If the EU and the WHO aspire to develop durable active ageing collectives, the type of collective at The Cordial Club should be taken into account. For a large group of older people, it is not physical activity, health or longevity that drives their everyday activities, but the cultural significance of the activity and the collective wherein it is embedded. In this regard, physical activity is merely an added benefit, although this benefit can prove to be highly important for the quality of life of these older people in the long run. The types of activities that have these qualities, of which billiards is merely one out of many, tend to be absent from active ageing initiatives. While this relates to the aforementioned hierarchy amongst activities, this hierarchy is dismissed at The Cordial Club. It requires a cultural analytical gaze on seemingly insignificant practices to see billiards as an active ageing activity. I have used the "kitchen entrance" approach in order to rearticulate what active ageing does to culturally specific forms of practice, and in order to compose a different type of active ageing and a different type of good old age. Billiards is out of sync with the active ageing discourse, but perhaps it should instead be highlighted as a way to anchor active ageing more firmly in everyday practices.

The out-of-sync-ness proposed in this article does not just relate to the object of the study, in this case billiards, but also to the researcher's presence in the field. My disruption of the rhythm in the game made this rhythm visible to me. My disruption made the invisible visible and revealed that, without my presence, billiards is a meticulously composed rhythm comprised of activity and passivity. Thus, the out-of-sync-ness is a way to make the seemingly insignificant visible, and I used my own out-of-sync-ness as an analytical tool to study the kitchen entrance. This analytical and methodological strategy could be transferred to other ethnological studies where the researcher is loudly and inescapably different from the collective that is being studied.

Notes

1 I would like to thank The Nordea Foundation for the funding of the research via the Centre for Healthy Ageing, University of Copenhagen. I would also like to thank the members of The Cordial Club, my co-supervisor Astrid P. Jespersen, Tiago Moreira and Marie Sandberg for their constructive comments, and the editors and reviewers for their comments to the manuscript.
2 Paradoxically Alan Walker, one of the intellectual craftsmen behind active ageing in the EU, is a former student of Peter Townsend, and was a key figure in the articulation of the theory of structured dependency in the late 1970s (e.g. Walker 1980). Together with Tiago Moreira, I analyse this productive relation between critical gerontology and active ageing policy as a circular process of negative feedback (Lassen & Moreira 2014).
3 The type of billiards played at The Cordial Club is a Danish version called "skomager" (cobbler). In this game, a player can score "skæve" (askew) points, when the red ball (used for shooting to the white balls) hits the pins or when other mistakes are made. The "skæve" points are then given to each of the other players.
4 All the names of the interviewees were changed to ensure confidentiality. Unless otherwise stated, all quotes are from interviews and translated from Danish by the author.
5 "Thingamajig" is the closest translation I could find of "plingeling", which is an expression often used to replace a word in a humorous manner. Here, "thingamajig" refers to Bent's pacemaker.

References

Angevaren, M., G. Aufdemkampe, H.J. Verhaar, A. Aleman & L. Vanhees 2008: Physical Activity and Enhanced Fitness to Improve Cognitive Function in Older People without Known Cognitive Impairment. *The Cochrane Library* 3.
Bendix, R.F., A. Eggert & A Peselmann 2012: Introduction:

Heritage Regimes and the State. In: R.F. Bendix, A. Eggert & A. Peselmann (eds.), *Heritage Regimes and the State*. Göttingen: Universitätsverlag Göttingen.

Biggs, S. & J.L. Powell, 2001: A Foucauldian Analysis of Old Age and the Power of Social Welfare. *Journal of Aging & Social Policy* 12:2, 1–20.

Boudiny, K. 2013: 'Active Ageing': From Empty Rhetoric to Effective Policy Tool. *Ageing and Society* 33:6, 1077–1098.

Cavan, R.S. 1949: *Personal Adjustment in Old Age*. Chicago: Science Research Associates Inc.

Christensen, K., G. Doblhammer, R. Rau & J.W. Vaupel 2009: Ageing Populations: The Challenges Ahead. *The Lancet* 374:9696, 1196–1208.

Clarke, A. & L. Warren 2007: Hopes, Fears and Expectations about the Future: What Do Older People's Stories Tell us about Active Ageing? *Ageing & Society* 27, 465–488.

Coleman, S. & P. Collins 2006: *Locating the Field: Space, Place and Context in Anthropology*. Oxford: Berg.

Damsholt, T. & D.G. Simonsen 2009: Introduktion. In: T. Damsholt, D.G. Simonsen & C. Mordhorst (eds.), *Materialiseringer*. Århus Universitetsforlag.

EC 2011: *How to Promote Active Ageing in Europe: EU Support to Local and Regional Actors*. Brussels: AGE Platform Europe & European Commission.

Ehn, B. & O. Löfgren 2006: *Kulturanalyser*. Århus: Klim.

Ekerdt, D.J. 1986: The Busy Ethic: Moral Continuity between Work and Retirement. *The Gerontologist* 26:3, 239–241.

Estes, C.L. & E.A. Binney 1989: The Biomedicalization of Aging: Dangers and Dilemmas. *The Gerontologist* 29:5, 587–596.

EU 2012: *Pension Adequacy in the European Union 2010–2050*. Luxembourg: European Union.

European Senior Citizens Union 2003: Do not Add Years to Life, but also Add Life to Years – as well as to People with Disabilities. Published online: http://www.eu-seniorunion.info/en/activities/projects/Leipzig-Life2years_disabled-enw.pdf. Accessed November 28, 2013.

Gomart, E. & A. Hennion 1999: A Sociology of Attachment: Music Amateurs, Drug Users. In: J. Law & J. Hassard, *Actor Network Theory and After*. Oxford: Wiley, pp. 220–247.

Havighurst, R.J. 1954: Flexibility and the Social Roles of the Retired. *American Journal of Sociology* 59:4, 309–311.

Havighurst, R.J. 1969: *Adjustment to Retirement: A Cross-National Study*. Assen: Van Gorcum.

Holstein, M.B. & M. Minkler 2007: Critical Gerontology: Reflections for the 21st century. In: M. Bernard & T. Scharf (eds.), *Critical Perspectives on Ageing Societies*. Bristol: Policy.

Jespersen, A.P. 2007: *Engagement i arbejdet? Konsultationsprocesser hos danske praktiserende læger*. Ph.D. dissertation. University of Copenhagen.

Jespersen, A.P., M.K. Petersen, C. Ren & M. Sandberg 2012: Guest Editorial: Cultural Analysis as Intervention. *Science Studies* 25:1, 3–12.

Katz, S. 1996: *Disciplining Old Age: The Formation of Gerontological Knowledge*. Charlottesville: University Press of Virginia.

Katz, S. 2000: Busy Bodies: Activity, Aging, and the Management of Everyday Life. *Journal of Aging Studies* 14:2, 135–152.

Katz, S. 2001: Growing Older without Aging? Positive Aging, Anti-Aging and Anti-Ageism. *Generations* 25:4, 27–32.

Lassen, A.J. 2014: Keeping Disease at Arm's Length: How Older Danish People Distance Disease through Active Ageing. *Ageing & Society*. Published online March 27, 2014: http://dx.doi.org/10.1017/S0144686X14000245.

Lassen, A.J. & T. Moreira 2014: Unmaking Old Age: Political and Cognitive Formats of Active Ageing. *Journal of Aging Studies* 30:1, 33–46.

Latour, B. 1987: *Science in Action: How to Follow Scientists and Engineers through Society*. Cambridge: Harvard University Press.

Latour, B. 1988: *The Pasteurization of France*. Cambridge: Harvard University Press.

Latour, B. 1991: Technology is Society made Durable. In: J. Law (ed.), *A Sociology of Monsters: Essays on Power, Technology and Domination*. London & New York: Routledge.

Michelon, L.C. 1954: The New Leisure Class. *American Journal of Sociology* 59:4, 371–378.

Moreira, T. 2004: Self, Agency and the Surgical Collective: Detachment. *Sociology of Health & Illness* 26:1, 32–49.

Moulaert, T. & M. Paris 2013: Social Policy on Ageing: The Case of "Active Ageing" as a Theatrical Metaphor. *International Journal of Social Science Studies* 1:2, 113–123.

Otto, L. 2005: Introduktion til forskningsfeltet. In: M. Kragelund & L. Otto (eds.), *Materialitet og dannelse – En studiebog*. Copenhagen: Danmarks Pædagogiske Forlag.

Pilgaard, M. 2009: *Sport og motion i danskernes hverdag*. Copenhagen: Idrættens Analyseinstitut.

Pollak, O. 1948: *Social Adjustment in Old Age: A Research Planning Report*. New York: Social Science Research Council.

Pressey, S.L. & E. Simcoe 1950: Case Study Comparisons of Successful and Problem Old People. *Journal of Gerontology* 5:2, 168–175.

Rowe, J.W. & R.L. Kahn 1987: Human Aging: Usual and Successful. *Science* 237:4811, 143–149.

Sandberg, M. 2009: *Grænsens nærvær og fravær: Europæiseringsprocesser i en tvillingeby* på den *polsk-tyske grænse*. Ph.D. dissertation. University of Copenhagen.

Schnohr, P. 1968: An Investigation of Previous Athletes: A Preliminary Communication. *The Journal of Sports Medicine and Physical Fitness* 8:4, 241–244.

Stenner, P., T. McFarquhar & A. Bowling 2011: Older People and 'Active Ageing': Subjective Aspects of Ageing Actively. *Journal of Health Psychology* 16:3, 467–477.

Sundhedsstyrelsen 2011: *Fysisk aktivitet – håndbog om forebyggelse og behandling*. Copenhagen: Sundhedsstyrelsen.

Townsend, J., M. Godfrey & T. Denby 2006: Heroines, Villains and Victims: Older People's Perceptions of Others. *Ageing & Society* 26, 883–900.

Townsend, P. 1981: The Structured Dependency of the Elderly: A Creation of Social Policy in the Twentieth Century. *Ageing & Society* 1, 5–28.

Venn, S. & S. Arber 2011: Day-Time Sleep and Active Ageing in Later Life. *Ageing & Society* 31, 197–216.

Walker, A. 1980: The Social Creation of Poverty and Dependency in Old Age. *Journal of Social Policy* 9:1, 49–75.

Walker, A. 2002: A Strategy for Active Ageing. *International Social Security Review* 55:1, 121–139.

Walker, A. 2006: Active Ageing in Employment: Its Meaning and Potential. *Asia-Pacific Review* 13:1, 78–93.

Welz, G. 2012: The Diversity of European Food Cultures. In: U. Kockel, M. Nic Craith & J. Frykman (eds.), *A Companion to the Anthropology of Europe*. Chichester, West Sussex, UK & Malden, MA: Wiley-Blackwell cop.

WHO 1996: *The Heidelberg Guidelines for Promoting Physical Activity among Older Persons – Guidelines Series for Healthy Ageing I*. Geneva: World Health Organization.

WHO 1998: *Growing Older – Staying Well: Ageing and Physical Activity in Everyday Life*. Geneva: World Health Organization.

WHO 1999: *Ageing: Exploding the Myths*. Geneva: World Health Organization.

WHO 2002: *Active Ageing: A Policy Framework*. Geneva: World Health Organization.

WHO 2008: *Older Persons in Emergencies: An Active Ageing Perspective*. Geneva: World Health Organization.

WHO: http://www.who.int/ageing/en/. Accessed November 28, 2013.

Zahrobsky, M.: 1950: Recreation Programs in Homes for the Aged in Cook County, Illinois. *The Social Service Review* 24:1, 41–50.

Zaidi, A., K. Gasior, M.M. Hofmarcher, O. Lelkes, B. Marin, R. Rodrigues, A. Schmidt, P. Vanhuysse & E. Zólyomi 2013: *Active Ageing Index 2012*. Vienna: European Centre.

Aske Juul Lassen is a Ph.D. student at the Centre for Healthy Ageing, Department of Ethnology, SAXO-Institute, University of Copenhagen. He specialises in cultural analysis, ethnography, humanistic health research, biopolitics, science and technology studies and user-driven innovation. Together with Julie Bønnelycke and Lene Otto he recently published "Innovating for 'Active Ageing' in a Public-Private Innovation Partnership: Creating Doable Problems and Alignment" (*Technological Forecasting and Social Change*, 2014: http://dx.doi.org/10.1016/j.techfore.2014.01.006). (ajlas@hum.ku.dk)

TRANSNATIONAL HERITAGE IN THE MAKING
Strategies for Narrating Cultural Heritage as European in the Intergovernmental Initiative of the European Heritage Label

Tuuli Lähdesmäki

The idea of a transnational cultural heritage has become topical in Europe because of the new EU heritage initiatives, such as the European Heritage Label scheme. Even though the scheme is administered at the European level, its implementation is transferred to heritage agents in the countries participating in the initiative. How do the heritage agents narrate the labeled heritage sites as European? Using the method of narrative analysis, this article identifies six key strategies of making sense of a European cultural heritage. Even though the scheme includes certain frameworks in which the heritage agents have to interpret and narrate the sites as European, it enables them to interpret the idea of Europe in their own way – and thus use their power to define a European identity.

Keywords: European Heritage Label, European identity, narration, nationalism, transnational cultural heritage

Since the 1980s culture has become an increasingly important domain on the EU's political agenda. A concrete result of this development is the establishment of various cultural initiatives and programs, which are governed by the EU but implemented at the local level. Besides strengthening cultural political aims, the EU has started to pay more and more attention to the cultural identity of its citizens and promotes their identification with Europe (Näss 2010; Stråth 2002; Shore 2000). In practice, discussions on culture and identity merge in the EU's cultural political rhetoric – a European identity or Europeanness is considered to be based on shared cultural roots and manifested through diverse cultural objects, sites, practices, and symbols.

In the current rhetoric of the EU's cultural policy, the common cultural heritage is given a particularly important role in the formation of a European identity. Several core EU documents, such as the Treaty of Lisbon, the European Agenda for Culture, and various decisions on cultural and civic programs, produce and foster the idea of a European identity by emphasizing the cultural heritage as a common layer of meanings shared by all Europeans (Lähdesmäki 2012). In the rhetoric of these documents, the cultural heritage in the EU member states is Europeanized – represented as European and as a part of a common European culture, history, and legacy.

During the past two decades the EU has launched or jointly administered several initiatives, such as the Raphael community action program (1997–2000), the European Heritage Days (in cooperation with the Council of Europe since 1999), and the European Union Prize for Cultural Heritage (since 2002), which focus on fostering the cultural heritage in Europe. The European Heritage Label (EHL) is the EU's most recent cultural initiative in this domain. The EHL was launched as an intergovernmental cultural scheme in 2006, initiated by the French Minister of Culture and Communication and supported by the Spanish and Hungarian ministers. Its main aim was to identify and designate sites which "have played a key role in building and uniting Europe" and to promote "a European reading of these sites" instead of their national interpretation (EC 2010: 15). The ideological and political motive for the EHL scheme was to turn the national heritage into a shared transnational European heritage which would function as a basis for "our" (European) identity and feeling of belonging, as the intergovernmental declaration on the EHL indicates:

We, the European Union Ministers for Culture participating in the European Heritage Label initiative: (---) Declare that our heritage in all its diversity is one of the most significant elements of our identity, our shared values and our principles. (---) Agree to promote the European nature of cultural assets and the sites which have shaped Europe's history, and to share and raise awareness of the wealth of European Heritage among its people. (Declaration on the initiative for a European Heritage Label 2007)

In 2007 the first series of sites (altogether 42, including, e.g., the Acropolis in Greece, the Cluny Abbey, and the house of Robert Schuman in France) were awarded with the label. The listings of possible EHL sites were first compiled at the national level by a committee of national heritage experts. The final decisions on the designations were made by the Heritage Committee of Europe, consisting of the Ministries of Culture and the European Commissioner for Culture or the latter's representatives. By 2011, 67 sites from 19 countries were awarded with the label. The countries that have participated in the intergovernmental scheme are: Belgium, Bulgaria, Cyprus, the Czech Republic, France, Germany, Greece, Hungary, Italy, Latvia, Lithuania, Malta, Poland, Portugal, Romania, Slovakia, Slovenia, Spain, and Switzerland.

The first years of the scheme indicated that the initiative was difficult to effectively implement on an intergovernmental basis due to the lack of common coordination and possibilities for operational arrangements (EC 2010: 18–20; MacCoshan et al. 2009). The implementation of the intergovernmental initiative was criticized for the lack of clear criteria for the label and the diversity of interpretations of the "European dimension" and "European significance" in the participating countries (MacCoshan et al. 2009: 18). The scheme was, however, considered important by the European Parliament and the European Council, and in 2008 the European Council adopted conclusions that transformed the initiative into an official EU action. In 2013 the EU-level action was launched with a two-year transitional phase after which it will turn into a regular action. The sites already awarded with the label during the intergovernmental phase have to reapply for the label during 2014 according to the new scheme and its clarified regulations.

Even though the EHL scheme has been administered at the European or transnational level, its implementation – defining and narrating sites as European and as emblematic of a European identity and promoting them as such – was transferred to heritage agents in the countries participating in the initiative. The agents and organizations that have nominated the sites for the label differ greatly from each other because of the diverse nature of the sites. In the case of museums or memorials, the agents represented their own institutions, such as museums or memorial foundations. In the case of broader heritage entities, such as city centers or larger archeological or environmental areas, the agents also included administrative authorities responsible for cultural matters in the city or region. The professional backgrounds of the agents were, thus, in the museum and heritage field, history, and cultural administration.

In this article[1] I explore the EHL initiative in its intergovernmental phase and investigate how "European reading" of the heritage sites was carried out within the framework of the scheme. The analysis in the article relies on a narrative approach which emphasizes narration as a social act and narratives as social products produced by people in different social, historical, and cultural contexts and positions (Czarniawska 2004). In the analysis narrating is perceived as an interpretive device through which people represent the world to both themselves and others. As Steph Lawler (2002: 242–243) points out, "narratives are central means with which people connect together past and present, self and other. They do so within the context of cultural narratives which delimit what can be said, what stories can be told, what will count as meaningful, and what will seem to be nonsensical." Thus, narratives are tools for empowering agencies and legitimizing cultural and social meanings. Even though narrative inquiry includes several different theoretical and methodological orientations, the analysis is based on the notion of the storied or narrativized nature of social interaction and reality – they are constructed and made sensible through processual and temporal narrative structures. Narratives have also been perceived as the key means through which people produce their identities (e.g., Ricoeur 1991); this also applies to collective identity processes such as the European project.

This investigation focuses on the local, regional, and national heritage agents and organizations and their narrative strategies and the rhetorical means used when interpreting and representing the heritage sites as European and as manifestations of a common European identity. In the article the different modes of argumentation in narrating the sites as European are called strategies in order to stress the political and ideological character of these modes. The term presumes that the eligible goal – in this case being European – can be achieved in several (even competing) ways, and that the use of a certain way – in this case a way of narrating a site as European – can be a strategic choice in order to achieve desirable ends with the available means (on the concept of strategy, see, e.g., Mckeown 2012; on narrative strategies, e.g., DuPlessis 1985; Bacchilega 1997; Vázques 2011). However, the rhetoric used in narrating Europeanness may be either intentional or unintentional, and certain types of narratives of Europeanness may result from both conscious and unconscious practices. The ideological and political motives of using the recognized strategies and rhetorical means are discussed in the final two sections of the article.

The research data consist of introductions to and descriptions of the 67 labeled sites on the official web pages of the intergovernmental EHL scheme (launched by the Spanish Ministry of Culture, which functioned as the secretariat of the scheme from 2008 to 2011) and 39 applications for the label available online. The introductions and descriptions of the sites are usually quotations or summaries of the application texts, particularly the responses to the key question in the application form which is: "How is this heritage site/object, which has played a key role in European history, emblematic of European identity?" In the form the applicants were advised to justify, on the basis of the selection criteria of the Heritage Committee of Europe, why the site should be given the EHL label. Besides having to demonstrate that they have stable management and administration structures as well as policies for improving and promoting the site and its artistic and cultural activities and that the site is rooted in existing international networks, the selection criteria expected the applicants to justify a "European and transnational dimension of the site," the "capacity of strengthening the European citizenship," and/or that the site in question played "a key role in understanding European history and culture" (The European Heritage Label, Rules of Procedure, Annex II 2007). Accordingly, such policy and preparatory documents of the intergovernmental initiative and the EU action were studied in order to understand the political and ideological bases of the EHL.

European Identity as Narrativization

In this article the conception of identity relies on its discursive and narrative nature. Following the views of Gerard Delanty and Chris Rumford (2005: 51), the role of language and the discursive and narrative point of departure are understood as being crucial in shaping identities. According to them, the fundamental basis of the conception of identity is in its processual and constructed nature: identities arise only in relation to social action. Discursive meaning-making processes and narrativization can be considered a form of social action in which diverse "mute" cultural phenomena are operationalized by language, turned into symbolic markers, functionalized as social practices, and related to certain social orders.

The concept of a European identity has been vibrantly discussed among scholars of European cultural processes (e.g., Kohli 2000; Stråth 2002; Delanty 2002; Herrmann & Brewer 2004; Bruter 2005; Pichler 2008; Antonsich 2008; Checkel & Katzenstein 2009; Risse 2010). As the discussions indicate, the idea of a European identity is profoundly complex and includes meanings which vary depending on the discursive situations in which the idea is being produced, defined, and used. In addition, the idea of a European identity is easily politicized at both national and European levels. The question about a European identity embodies both distinguishable, yet in several ways overlapping dimensions of the collective and the individual. Agents shaping the collective discourse on a European identity take a very prominent position on how identity crystallizes at the

individual level (Bee 2008). During the past decades, the European Commission has been an active agent in the construction of a European identity. Several civic and cultural initiatives of the EU – often formulated through long-term collaborative processes – have aimed at providing meanings for Europe, the EU, and a European identity for EU citizens (e.g., Bruter 2003; van Bruggen 2006). As the EHL scheme indicates, diverse local, regional, and national agents participate (or are "forced" to participate because attendance in the EU's civic and cultural initiatives obliges them to participate) in the meaning-making of Europe, the EU, and a European identity.

The cultural emphasis on the conception of a European identity has often been interpreted as a thick version of it, appealing to (real or imagined) shared features and qualities, while the thin version of a European identity refers to the ideas of constitutional patriotism and a cosmopolitan notion of a European identity (Beck & Grande 2007; Pichler 2008, 2009). The EU's cultural initiatives, such as the EHL, promote the thick notion of a European identity by adopting the ideas of a common culture and heritage as their fundamental elements. Cultural phenomena, collective symbols, historical narrations, and memories and material remnants of the past are affective matters and thus profoundly sensitive, albeit effective, instruments for political and ideological attempts to create a feeling of belonging, communality, and a common identity. The cultural phenomena, symbols, histories, and memories do not, however, turn into the elements of identity building just by themselves; they have to be given collective meanings to become resources for collective identities. Thus, discursive meaning-making processes and narrativization are integral constituents of the collective identity-building process.

Identities are often produced and manifested in order to distinguish oneself from "others" and to indicate one's belonging to a particular community. In this sense, the relation to the conception of a national culture or national identity is essential to the production of Europeanness.

The transforming and fluid relations of national and European identification have been much discussed (e.g., Herrmann & Brewer 2004; Risse 2010). On the one hand, a European identity can be perceived as being produced as a negation of or a reaction to a national or non-European identity. On the other hand, a European identity is perceived as complementary to the national, regional, and local identities of people living in Europe (Breakwell 2004; Risse 2006). The distinction of the different identities or the distinct layers of an identity, as well as the idea of a fusion or a merging of different identities, are discursively and narratively produced and operationalized in language. Particularly the complex, fluid, and unsettled conceptions of identities, such as a European identity, are discursive spaces within which their meanings are constantly and continuously negotiated. Thus, as Monica Sassatelli (2009: 14) has noticed, a European identity increasingly takes on a language of becoming, rather than that of a stable and monolithic being.

When a European identity is perceived as a discursive, narrative, and linguistic construction which is in an ongoing state of becoming (as is the case in this article), its production can be considered as being based on some narrative modes and models. These modes and models are being produced, e.g., by the media, politicians, and academia. One profoundly influential producer and establisher of certain narrative modes of defining a European identity is the EU's cultural policy rhetoric. It is at the same time a fundamental political dimension of the EU's policy rhetoric – certain modes and models of narrating a European identity are represented as natural, true, and correct and as modes which are expected to be followed at the national, regional, and local levels. Public narratives are powerful in structuring what can be said and, conversely, in foreclosing certain meanings (Lawler 2002: 252). In addition to the EU's policy rhetoric, national history writing and popular and public histories offer strong narrative modes and models for perceiving and representing a European identity, as the analysis indicates.

Strategies of Narrating Cultural Heritage as European in the EHL Scheme

The EHL applications and the descriptions of the labeled sites on the official web pages of the scheme relied on a thick understanding of a European identity: the heritage agents usually narrated it as a cultural identity based on a common history, shared cultural roots, and a specific mental state. Following the instructions of the EHL scheme, the underlying principle in the data was to represent the (previously) locally, regionally, or nationally recognized and interpreted sites, monuments, historical incidents, and persons as European. The attempts to Europeanize the local, regional, or national *loci memoriae* could be, e.g., expressed in the data as an opportunity to broaden the local, regional, or national significance of a heritage to the European level, and as a generous act of sharing a national heritage with the rest of the Europeans, as the following quotation from the German EHL application for the Reformation network indicates:

> The initiative is also the next public step in an approach which, as European 'Lieux de Mémoire', has already been widely discussed in an academic context, both the perspective of the formation of a European consciousness in the past, and in the hope of developing a clearer European identity in the future. This would appear to be an opportune time to create a network of German loci memoriae of the Reformation as a locus memoriae we can all share. (Sites of the Reformation network 2010: 1–2)

In addition to the Europeanization of local, regional, and national phenomena, the data included a reverse narrative principle in which the features and phenomena perceived as European were considered to be manifested in the local, regional, or national environment. The localization or nationalization of European phenomena was utilized in the data, e.g., by emphasizing the adaptation of "European" architectural or artistic movements and way of life into the local or national environment, as the following quotation from the Bulgarian EHL application for the city center of Rousse illustrates:

> All urban sites suggested for listing under the European Heritage Label Scheme belong to a group of sites in the central city zone. It presents not only the Rousse's unique atmosphere, but also demonstrates the successful integration of European cultural identity, architectural trends and lifestyle into the national tradition. (The historic and architectural ensemble of Rousse City Centre 2007: 5)

A closer analysis of the data brought to the fore six strategies of narrating the labeled sites as European. Identification of these strategies was based on the researcher's comparison between narrative patterns and meaning-making processes present in the data. In practice, the different narrative strategies were often merged or combined in the rhetoric of the EHL applications and the descriptions of the sites on the official web pages. All the strategies comprise more concrete rhetorical means through which the strategies are linguistically operationalized. Some of the strategies obey – and thus participate in promoting and strengthening – the narrative modes used by the EU in its policy rhetoric. Some other strategies follow the narrative modes traditionally used in national history writing or in more popular situations of making sense of the past. The strategies, the rhetorical means, the sources of narrative modes, and the notions on a European identity related to each strategy are summarized in Table 1.

Narrative Strategy of European-wide Interaction
One of the most common strategies of narrating the sites' Europeanness in the data was to emphasize the European-wide interaction of people and ideas that were perceived as characterizing the labeled site, its history, or the present condition. The strategy follows the EU's policy rhetoric used in diverse cultural and civic programs, which emphasizes the importance of fostering transnational and cross-border cooperation, interaction, and dialog between the member states, regions, organizations, and individuals in Europe. In the data, a common rhetorical means of this strategy was to list the (current) European countries from where the artists, architects, or stylistic influences arrived at the site in question, as the Polish EHL application for the Cathedral of St. Wenceslas and St. Stanislaus illustrates:

> The European importance of Wawel Cathedral is confirmed not only by historical background but also by its artistic values. Many European architects and artists from Italy, Russia, France, Germany, Austria or Denmark attended the building and decorating of the Cathedral. One can recognize distinct signs of particular periods in which several artworks of great significance in European art were created. (Cathedral of St. Wenceslas and St. Stanislaus on Wawel Hill in Cracow 2007: 2)

Besides the broad involvement of artists, architects, and stylistic movements from different European countries, the Europeanness and the European significance of the sites were often narrated by using rhetorical means of emphasizing the European-wide influence or the broad distribution of the ideas or goods produced at the site. The description of the Belgium Raeren Pottery Museum on the EHL web pages illustrates this means:

> Today these objects are preserved not only in the place where they were produced, in the Raeren Pottery Museum, but also in the most important European museums (the Louvre, the MRAH in Brussels, the Victoria & Albert Museum in London, the Rijksmuseum in Amsterdam, and museums of decorative arts in Berlin, Vienna, Budapest, Frankfurt, Hamburg, Cologne, Munich, etc.). (EHL 2013a)

The EU's current political rhetoric stresses – in line with the official slogan of the EU – both unity and diversity as the main features of a European cultural identity: European culture(s) are seen as being characterized both by shared cultural roots and as distinct cultural units. In the data, the narration of the sites' Europeanness often followed the idea of "unity in diversity" by utilizing a rhetorical means of emphasizing the site as a meeting point of diverse peoples, nations, and ethnic and religious groups. The former socialist countries typically emphasized their sites as meeting points of the East and the West, or the West and the Balkans. In the Southern European and Mediterranean countries the sites were often narrated as meeting points of Europe, Africa, and Asia, while the countries in Central Europe emphasized their sites as crossroads of Northern and Southern Europe. Europeanness was narrated in the data as a flourishing and culturally stimulating national and ethnic pluralism that originates from the distant past of the continent. In addition, many of the labeled sites narrated their Europeanness through being a confluence of mercantile routes, as the description of the Swiss Hospice of St. Gothard illustrates:

> The St. Gothard Pass and its emblematic Hospice have always formed a link between Northern and Southern Europe. Known to have been used since the 3rd century BCE, from the 13th century on it became the required route for merchants, with the conditions needed for regular traffic. The St. Gothard has become an emblem of modern European mobility and all its aspects. (EHL 2013b)

As the previous quotation indicates, the means of emphasizing the site as a meeting point of diverse people reflects the EU's current policy rhetoric on the free movement of people and goods. In the data, the "meeting" of different nations and ethnic groups was typically represented as a positive incident that generated a dynamic and creative atmosphere during the different historical phases of the site, even though the "meeting" would have included armed conflicts, combats, or con-

quests of rival powers. The sites' violent history as a stage of continuous conquests by neighboring rulers could be softened in the data by narrating the history as an indication of the strategic significance of the site and the consequences of the conquests as the rich historical multilayeredness of the site. In general, in the strategy the notion of a European identity relied on the idea of more or less distinct national identities: distinct peoples and nations in Europe have their own historical experiences and trajectories which are, however, interactive and interdependent but still separated. European identity was narrated as an ensemble of the national identities in Europe.

Narrative Strategy of Cultural Grandeur

The rhetoric of popular and public history often praises and glorifies the most well-known heritage and touristic sites in Europe, and thus reproduces their role in the canon of important European monuments and architectural constructions. Bringing to the fore their grandeur and exclusiveness is a typical way to describe their significance. The strategy of cultural grandeur was often used in the data to justify the EHL sites' Europeanness. The strategy was operationalized through a rhetorical means of emphasizing the outstanding quality, beauty, or splendor of the sites, particularly in cases of palaces, castles, and churches.

In academia, historical artistic styles and architectural movements have also been perceived as emblematic features that penetrate the history and culture of Europe and transcend the particularism of national cultures (e.g., Delanty & Jones 2002: 453–454). In addition, the EU has utilized the idea of a common European architectural heritage in its attempts to create common EU symbols – the Euro banknote designs, for example, illustrate different architectural motifs associated with the history of Europe. In the data, the European dimension of the sites was often narrated by using the rhetorical means of emphasizing the exemplary character of the sites in relation to "European" architectural styles. Thus, for example, the Cluny Abbey in France was described as "a leading disseminator of the Romanesque style and of Gregorian Reform" (EHL 2013c), and the Rundale Palace in Latvia as "a prime exponent of European Renaissance and Baroque culture" (EHL 2013d). In addition, the labeled sites included several monuments and museums of composers and artists. In the rhetoric of the data, references to traditional forms of high culture, such as opera, classical music, and fine art, were related to European cultural specificity. The strategy of narrating the sites' Europeanness through the strategy of cultural grandeur reflects the notion of the European identity as a supranational (high) cultural identity.

Narrative Strategy of Transnational Ideas

In the data, the labeled EHL sites were often narrated as European by bringing to the fore diverse transnational ideas represented as being derived from shared European values and societal principles. Emphasizing these ideas can be identified as a rhetorical means of defining the site as European. The most often repeated ideas in the data were: democracy, rights, and freedoms (such as individual and group rights and freedom of expression, speech, and association); coexistence of people, mutual respect, and equality between nations; and humanitarian spirit, solidarity, and peace. Referring to these ideas was used in the data as a justification for the European significance of the sites, as the following description of the mausoleum and birthplace of General Milan Rastislav Štefánik in Slovakia illustrates:

He was a man who influenced European politics with his outstanding diplomatic efforts, and whose ideas and actions entitle him to be considered the "first European". He believed that one day peace and harmony would finally reign among European nations, and called this "Europeanisation". Equally dedicated to his own country, his mausoleum contains not only his tomb but the monument erected in his memory. It is an exceptional monument of European grandeur and symbol of the love, reverence and gratitude the Slovak and Czech people feel towards this extraordinary leader. (EHL 2013e)

The strategy reflects the EU's political rhetoric, which promotes the identified ideas as the fundamental European basis of the union. As, for example, the Treaty of Lisbon declares, it has been created by "drawing inspiration from the cultural, religious, and humanist inheritance of Europe, from which have developed the universal values of the inviolable and inalienable rights of the human person, freedom, democracy, equality, and the rule of law" and "desiring to deepen the solidarity between their peoples while respecting their history, their culture and their traditions" (Treaty of Lisbon 2008: article 1). As the treaty indicates, the EU's political rhetoric aims to outline the common values and mental background of Europe and to explain Europe as the home of democratic principles and a sense of justice. Thus, appealing to these values and societal ideas politicizes the narration of the Europeanness of the cultural heritage.

The data included several sites that were narrated as European by emphasizing ideas of entrepreneurship, worker mobility, and free trade. This rhetorical means was often utilized with more or less direct references to EU policy aims in the economic sector, as the following description of the industrial city of Zlin in the Czech Republic illustrates:

The most important point in terms of European identity is the Bat'a family's idea of a free market which, in the context of the period, was marked by tariffs and economic barriers, thus their project represented a major advance. To launch the project, they did not export the finished product but rather the whole industry complex, or in other words, the industrial cities created according to the Zlín model.

It also emphasises the idea of the free circulation of people, which is an equally important contribution to European identity. Young entrepreneurs came from all over the country and had an opportunity to attain their goals there, and in the future they would carry the ideas of Bat'a as their ambassadors around the world. (EHL 2013f)

The labeled sites comprise several churches, monasteries, and other religious buildings. Their European dimension was sometimes defined in the data by locating Christianity and Christian ethics as a common mental ground for a European identity. Christianity was narrated as a unifying history and a shared legacy of the continent that determines its current values, as the description of Saint Margaret's Church and Saint George's Church in Slovakia indicates:

> Both Saint Margaret's Church and Saint George's Church, which dates back to the 10th century, stand as testimony to a timeless and unifying phenomenon which has had a fundamental influence on the creation of modern day Europe: Christianity. (EHL 2013g)

Defining Christianity as a part of a common European heritage has been problematized in various political discussions. The modern "EU Europe" supported by the so-called European elites (Bruter 2005) relies on secular interpretations of a European identity and heritage, while the "conservative and nationalist Europe" attaches the Christian heritage and legacy to its idea of a European identity. The latter view has also been utilized in the political rhetoric of nationalist and populist strivings in several European countries willing to draw boundaries against Islam and Asian or African "cultures" (Risse 2010: 6). The struggles over formulating the preamble of the current EU's constitutional treaty indicated the contradictions between these two notions of Europe and a European identity. The suggested reference to God is not mentioned in the Treaty of Lisbon, but the "religious inheritance of Europe" is declared as a common foundation for the union in the endorsed version of the treaty. In general, the emphasis on transnational ideas in narrating the EHL sites as European reflects the notion of a European identity as a value identity – an identity based on ethical and moral principles.

Narrative Strategy of Anticipation of European Integration

Even though the EU policy rhetoric emphasizes both unity and diversity as the fundamental elements of the union and its goals, attempts to produce a stronger cohesion in the union – be the approach cultural, civic, political, or economic – seem to dominate the political discourse of the EU. As the underlying political and ideological aim of the union, the idea of unity penetrates the rhetoric of all the major political documents, determining also the policy rhetoric of the EHL. According to the data, the EU's idea of and aim for multilevel cohesion and unity in Europe was often utilized as a narrative strategy to define the Europeanness of the heritage sites. The sites were introduced as materialized evidence of historical strivings to create unity and cohesion between different nations, states, regions, and ethnic and religious groups in Europe. A common rhetorical means in this strategy was to narrate the labeled sites as historical anticipations of EU integration. In the data, the historical incidents, trajectories, and aims of former rulers were often described by identifying similarities between them and the current political and social conditions of the union, as the following quotation from the Spanish EHL application for the Monastery of San Jeronimo de Yuste illustrates:

> The Monastery of Yuste embraces a number of different characteristics relating to its European vocation. First of all, the Europe that Charles V yearned for and was on the verge of achieving, is very much in line with the values of western culture. His legacy provides the frame of reference by which to comprehend our shared history the feeling of spirituality which goes hand-in-hand with a way of viewing the world. Four-hundred years later, this legacy

remains intact in Yuste and has been realised through a series of advances such as the ECSC, the Treaty of Rome, the European Economic Community and the European Union. A veritable outpouring of responses to the dream that Charles V had when he relinquished the throne. (Monastery of San Jeronimo de Yuste 2007: 2)

The connection between history and present-day social and cultural conditions could also be brought to the fore in the data by interpreting similarities between the mental atmosphere of the past before the rise of the nation-states and the current social and cultural reality in Europe characterized by the post-national climate. The phases of history when national sentiments and identities did not yet determine people's feelings of belonging were compared to the people's (assumed) feelings in today's Europe. Similarities between people's past and current mobility and the flexibility of cultural and economic migratory flows could also be used as a rhetorical means to justify the EHL sites' Europeanness, as the following quotation from the Spanish EHL application for the Archive of the Crown of Aragon indicates:

> The ACA's documentary collections and the very existence of the Cultural Centre, go back to the origins of Europe, to a time in history when the region was taking shape from a political and culture point of view. This context, when national identities were not yet fully formed (the time when the Archive of the Crown of Aragon was instituted whose history is traced at this Centre), is strikingly similar to that of today because cultural and economic migratory flows between European countries during the Full and Lower Middle Ages was much more flexible than during later centuries thus reinforcing a sense of belonging to Europe. (Archive of the Crown of Aragon 2007: 14)

Besides narrating the historical incidents and heritage sites as predecessors of European integration in the twentieth century, some sites utilized a more straightforward rhetorical means of narrating the site as a part of the history of the EU. In this means the building of the EU and of Europe was often paralleled, as the description of Robert Schuman's House in France illustrates:

> In 1924 Robert Schuman, considered one of the "fathers of Europe", bought a house in Scy-Chazelles, on the outskirts of Metz. This house now has great symbolic value for the history of Europe and is the home of the Robert Schuman European Centre, which honours his memory while organising cultural and educational activities publicising his work and the way in which Europe was built and continues to develop. (EHL 2013h)

In the strategy of anticipation of European integration, the notion of a European identity parallels the political EU identity which emphasizes the union, its integration policies, and EU citizenship as common ground for a feeling of belonging. This may have a practical background motive: in order to be awarded with an EU-related initiative, the local, regional, and national agents may have sought to interpret the Europeanness of the sites in relation to the EU's core policies and the building of the EU.

Narrative Strategy of Self-Evidence

The ideological starting point of the EHL scheme is in the existence of a shared European cultural heritage and a common European identity for which the heritage functions as a building resource. In the data, the existence of a transnational heritage and a European identity were not questioned or problematized – on the contrary, they were often perceived as *a priori* entities. The *a priori* nature of a European identity could be utilized in narrating and justifying the Europeanness of the EHL sites. The sites were often simply introduced as European heritage and as indications of a European identity without more analytical or explanatory arguments. According to the logic of this narrative strategy, for example, the archeological site of Kourion in Cyprus could be narrated as "by definition a European monument" (Kourion 2007: 3), and the historical past of the Szigetvár Castle in Hungary as "known all over Europe" (Szigetvár Castle 2009: 4). In this narrative strategy, the Europeanness of the sites relied on the receivers' knowledge of history and culture and their ability to locate the sites in the European framework. When the sites were just declared European, their justification as such was difficult to deny – inability to perceive the site's Europeanness would have meant that the receiver was not familiar with European history and cultural and social phenomena.

In popular and public histories, antiquity and pre-historical and ancient archeological sites in particular are often introduced as having European significance and carrying a European historical and cultural legacy by simply existing and surviving through time. In the data, the sites with a long history were often automatically considered as European and as cradles of civilization in Europe. The further back the history of the sites went, the more obvious their nature as a common heritage and shared legacy became.

Strategy of Elevation of the Nation
Even though the focus of the EHL scheme is on the European dimension of the cultural heritage, a common approach to the labeled sites in the data was to view and discuss them within the national framework – as a part of national history, national culture, and crucial moments of the nation-building processes. For example, the Krakow Cathedral in Poland was described on the web pages of the scheme as "a great protagonist of Polish history" and the Szigetvar Castle in Hungary was emphasized in the EHL application as "a national symbol" related to the country's heroic national history, as the following quotations indicate:

This cathedral is inextricably linked to the history of the Polish nation, both in times of splendour and in times of adversity. As a great protagonist of Polish history, it was here that the Great Dukes and Kings of Poland were crowned; it was also the Royal Vault from the 11th to 18th century. (EHL 2013k)

The castle is a national symbol of tragic perseverance against the invading Turkish armies, which substantially outnumbered the defending Hungarian forces. In 1566, when it was no longer possible to continue to defend the castle, led by the Croatian-born Miklós Zrínyi, the defending battlers "dashed out" of the castle only to meet their destiny in the heroic assault they launched on the Turks. This act of heroism was later on many times commemorated both in Croatian and Hungarian literature as well as in several works of fine art. (Szigetvar Castle 2007: 2)

Rather than Europeanizing the national or nationalizing the European, many of the EHL applications and descriptions of the sites on the official web pages sought to elevate the nation and various national issues related to the sites in question. For example, the works of Lithuanian artist Milkalojus Konstantinas Ciurlionis were described on the web pages of the EHL scheme as follows:

Milkalojus Konstantinas Ciurlionis (1875–1911) born in Pustelnik (Marki) close to Varsovia was a painter and composer and is broadly held to be the most famous Lithuanian artist. (---) The majority of his paintings are housed at the M. K. Ciurlionis National Art Museum in Kaunas, Lithuania. His works have had a profound influence on modern Lithuanian culture. So important is his work that an asteroid, the 2420 Ciurlionis, was named after him. (EHL 2013j)

The narrative modes in the texts reflected national history writing. The texts emphasized the particularity of the nation or nation-state and its historical trajectories, achievements, and significance among other nations and nation-states in Europe. On the one hand, this kind of narrative strategy can be perceived as dismissing the European dimension due to its main interest in national-level issues. On the other hand, it can be perceived as a special mode of narrating and understanding Europeanness – a mode which relies on the idea of the Europe of nations, a combination of different nation-states with their own national identities, histories, cultural features, and heritage sites. In the framework of this narrative strategy, awarding nationally important sites with the EHL could be interpreted as official recognition of the significance of the nation and the national cultural and historical particularities in relation to other nations in Europe.

The strategy of elevating the nation was used particularly in relation to sites in the former socialist countries, such as Hungary, Bulgaria, Slovakia, Lithuania, and Poland. Besides nationally important buildings in Bulgaria and the Czech Republic, the labeled sites included memorials of national heroes, as the EHL application for the Vassil Levski Memorial Complex in Bulgaria indicates:

Vassil Levski, born Vassil Ivanov Kunchev (July 18th 1837–February 19th 1873), was a Bulgarian revolutionary, ideologist, strategist and theoretician of the Bulgarian national revolution and leader of the struggle for liberation from Ottoman rule. Due to his major significance for the liberation of Bulgaria, Vassil Levski is hailed as a national hero and often referred to as "The Apostle of Freedom" by the Bulgarian people. He is one of the most significant political men of the 19th century. ("Vassil Levski" Memorial Complex 2007: 1)

In fact, descriptions of the sites in the data could even focus on fostering the national identity as a justification for the label, as the following quotation from the EHL application for the Reformed College and the Great Church in Debrecen, Hungary, illustrates:

The Great Church is also an active player in the organisation of religious world congresses, and has served as the venue of the meeting of Hungarian minority Reformed Churches from the neighbouring countries on many occasions. These meetings are attended not only by Hungarians living in the Carpathian Basin but also by Reformed Hungarians living in Europe, and what is more, by several hundred visitors from overseas countries. These meetings evidence the diversity of the roles the Great Church plays in uniting different Hungarian communities all over and in facilitating the preservation of their Hungarian identity. (The Reformed College and the Great Church in Debrecen 2007: 6)

The paradoxical rhetorical means of narrating the "European dimension" of the sites by emphasizing their role in the national identity can also be understood as a reflection of the ideology of diversity present within current EU policy. Justifying the European dimension of the EHL sites by bringing to the fore the national identity relies on a nationalist interpretation of the EU's policy rhetoric which, in addition to unity, emphasizes the importance of fostering multilevel diversity in Europe. Thus, in this framework, the nurturing of national cultures and identities can be interpreted as the promotion of cultural diversity in Europe.

Narration of Cultural Heritage as Rethinking Europeanness

Heritage as an object, a concept, and a social practice inevitably includes a political dimension, and it is thus easily instrumentalized for use in diverse ideological and political projects. The idea of heritage is inseparable from the emergence of national identities and cultures and the development of the nation-state (Hobsbawm 1983: 6–7; Ashworth, Graham & Tunbridge 2005: 26–31; Mitchell 2001; Peckham 2003; Risse 2003). Many of the institutions through which heritage is still currently promoted and administered in European societies have played a crucial role in the nation-building processes. Can the idea of a heritage be transformed to the transnational European level? The EU's heritage politics has its ideological basis in the pan-Europeanist idea of a transnational heritage that transcends national and regional memory and history. As in the case of Unesco and its universalistic reading of history (Starzmann 2008; Kirshenblatt-Gimblett 2006; Di Cesari 2010), the rhetoric of the EU's heritage politics elevates the categories of ownership, access, and inheritance to transnational values, while the heritage sites become a "common good" belonging to all Europeans. As Nic Craith (2012: 19) has pointed out, despite the constant affirmation of a common European heritage, the notions of it lack conceptual integrity and vary with the location and the occasion. The EHL scheme is the EU's political attempt to produce transnational *lieux de mémoire* in a sense of Pierre Nora (1996) – institutionalized and materialized places and phenomena which (aim to) function on a European scale as symbolic elements of self-understanding and the collective memory of a community.

In academic discussions, scholars have had contradicting views on whether a transnational European heritage can eventually exist and if so, what might be its common ground (see, e.g., Ashworth & Larkham 1994). Some scholars have asked whether a common European cultural dimension that is not based on "a mere sum of national icons" (Monica Sassatelli 2006: 29) could even exist. Some others, such as Gerard Delanty (2009: 37), have questioned the possibility of common European commemoration and heritage practices due to the lack of a coherent "European people" – which is the main difference between Europe and its nations. As several scholars have pointed out, instead of supplanting national or state identities, the EU's attempts at cultural Europeanization have mobilized domestic resistance and opposition (Checkel & Katzenstein 2009; Jones & Subotic 2011: 542). The national emphasis in the EHL applications can be interpreted as reflecting these sentiments and thus as being domestic resistance inside the EHL agenda towards the Europeanization of culture.

Some scholars have found possible common ground for a European identity and transnational heritage in urbanity (Sassatelli 2009), European cities and their historical environment (Ashworth & Graham 1997), and the architectural styles and movements in Europe (Delanty & Jones 2002). The selection of EHL sites seems to support these urban approaches: most of the labeled sites are historical architectural monuments located in former or present-day cities. As Gerard Delanty (2002) has suggested, a common European identity could be based on a common "historical memory" which is related to Europe in a broader sense. There are incidents within European history that are not only national, but European, such as diverse religious conflicts, class-based confrontations, and wars that have had an impact across Europe. The conflicts and their traumas and reconciliations could function as a shared history in Europe and as a base for sentiments of communality. During recent years, several scholars have recognized a new European culture of apologies, mourning, and collective guilt for past war crimes and collective acts of violence (Delanty & Rumford 2005: 98; Cunningham 1999). Even though the applications and descriptions of the labeled EHL sites brought to the fore losses and terrors of the twentieth century wars in Europe, only two sites – the Franja Partisan Hospital and the Memorial Church of the Holy Spirit, both in Slovenia – focused more explicitly on remembering the victims of WWI and WWII.

Different nationalities may interpret "Europeanness" or "European" very differently (Risse 2003: 77; Jones & Subotic 2011: 254). For some nationalities a European identity is based on civic or political understanding, while some others emphasize its cultural notion (Bruter 2005). Moreover, several cultural value surveys among Europeans have indicated that the definitions of national heritage and European heritage vary considerably from one country to another (*Eurobarometer* 2007; Ipsos 2007). The EHL applications also revealed the different ways the idea and the concept of heritage are understood in different countries. For example, Latvia's applications emphasized authenticity and originality as core values of heritage, while in

Cyprus' applications historical multilayeredness functioned as the basis for the concept. Similarly, the idea of a transnational heritage got profoundly diverse emphases in different countries. In Spanish applications, for example, the sites were mainly discussed with reference to Europe and Europeanness, while in Hungary, national and nationalist discourse dominated the rhetoric.

In writing the history of Europe, there has been a noticeable bias in favor of Western and Southern Europe compared to Northern and Eastern Europe (Mälksoo 2009: 673). The EU's eastern expansions in 2004 and 2007 have forced the EU to face new memory regimes, which are forcefully entering the discourse competition taking place in the European public sphere. Due to the rearrangement of EU geography, the experiences of crimes of Communist regimes and the restriction of freedoms under socialist rule broaden or are expected to broaden the common narration of the recent history of Europe (Onken 2007: 30). The attempts of the Eastern and Central European countries to bring their mnemonic culture into the common European historical consciousness challenge the long-term tendency of the Western core of the EU to act as a model for the whole of Europe (Mälksoo 2009: 673). Culture has become one of the crucial arenas of political struggle in the countries' attempts to become European and narrate their belonging to Europe. The analysis indicates that the former socialist countries used the EHL scheme as an instrument to introduce their historical phases, cultural characteristics, arts, national heroes, and cities and raise their significance on the European scale. Seven countries suggested the label for persons, and five of these countries were former socialist countries. Among the labeled sites there are seven cities or city centers, six of which are located in former socialist countries. In the application texts these countries often sought to raise the awareness and significance of their regions, as the case of Riga illustrates: "The history of Riga, the Latvian capital, is the history of an important region of Europe: the Baltic territories" (EHL 2013i).

Conclusions

The foundations of European integration policies are in cooperation in the core areas of the EU, that is, economy and trade. The economic aspect is intertwined with EU policy discourses in various policy domains including culture and heritage-making. Cultural integration is, thus, grounded in political and economic integration in the EU. EU heritage politics is closely intertwined with economic aims: boosting cultural tourism, strengthening cultural industries, and enabling regional development. During the past couple of decades the EU has, however, attempted to legitimize itself as a cultural entity. As Cris Shore (1993: 785–786) has noted, an emphasis of the EU as a humanistic enterprise based on various social virtues and common cultural roots and identity can be perceived as having functional utility: it is a tool for promoting the EU's political legitimacy as well as attempts to bring the different member states together. The fundamental utility of this emphasis is in its affective nature: it appeals to the people's feelings of belonging, cultural and social attachments, communality, and collective values, and thus aims to justify the promotion of cultural integration in the EU. Along with this emphasis, heritage has become an important political arena in the EU's policy discourses.

The EHL scheme functions as one of the EU's ideological devices for creating and implementing a European-wide identity and heritage politics. As a political tool, the EHL scheme obeys one of the EU's fundamental principles of governance: it mingles the top-down and bottom-up dynamics between the EU and the local agents. This form of governance is also used in other EU actions and programs, such as the European Capital of Culture designation (Sassatelli 2006: 30). Through this kind of principle of governance the local agents are committed to building a common European identity and the EU as a cultural project. As indicated, the EHL scheme directs and instructs the local-, regional-, and national-level heritage agents to narrate themselves as European and thus participate in the production of a common European heritage, seemingly on their own initiative. The narrative modes of defining European and a European identity that are emphasized and promoted in the EU policy rhetoric were often repeated by the local, regional, and national agents. It signifies the powerful position of the EU in the European identity project.

However, the ideological and political agenda of the EHL scheme is not utilized only at the EU level; the scheme has taken advantage of the local, regional, and national levels to raise European or international awareness and the publicity of the heritage sites, attract domestic and international tourists, and promote the sites' possibilities to receive European and national funding, etc. The advantages of the label for the tourism industry undoubtedly motivate the local and national agents to implement the scheme. In general, the EHL scheme functions at the local, regional, and national levels as an instrument in the politics of European significance. Even though the EHL scheme includes certain frameworks in which the local, regional, and national agents have to interpret and narrate the sites as European, the scheme enables the agents to interpret the idea of Europe and Europeanness in their own way – and thus use their narrative power to define a European identity. This power was used, for example, to nationalize the European agenda of the EHL scheme – particularly in the former socialist countries – as the analysis of the article indicates. The empowering nature of narratives explains the relative ineffectiveness of European heritage-making as an integrative tool in Europe; the European agenda of the scheme could narrow to a national agenda. Transnational heritage policies, such as the EHL scheme and the Unesco World Heritage Listing, do not eventually transfer the power over heritage-making to the transnational or international heritage bodies. As in the case of the EHL scheme, the Unesco World Heritage listing is based on the national heritage agents and states, who imple-

ment the heritage policies on the national level (Bendix, Eggert & Peselmann 2012). As Chiara Bortolotto (2012: 277) has noticed, each state translates key terms of the Unesco Convention in different ways, resulting in "domestication of global standards". A similar practice takes place within the EHL scheme.

During the past two decades academic discussions have emphasized the idea of a "Europe of regions" to describe the phenomena where "the 'European' is becoming increasingly 'localized', and simultaneously, the 'local' is clearly being 'Europeanized'" (Johler 2002: 9). In this process, nations and nationalities have been predicted to lose their previous position while regions are considered to be gaining new importance. However, some scholars have noticed that the phrase has eventually been much more a tool of governance "from above" than a tool for regionalism "from below" (Paasi 2009: 478). The analysis of the EHL scheme indicates that Europe is still mainly interpreted and understood as the Europe of nations. The distinct nations and nation-states with their particular national identities, cultures, and histories are perceived as the key players in the formation of Europe and its identity.

The analysis of the EHL applications and the descriptions of the labeled sites on the official web pages of the scheme brought to the fore six strategies of narrating the sites as European. The change of the scheme from an intergovernmental initiative into an EU action with a unified administration and reformulated selection criteria and rules may influence the strategies of narrating European cultural heritage within the framework of the scheme in the future. The narratives of Europeanness in different countries reflect the constant social, cultural, economic, and political transformations in Europe, and are thus fluid and processual. Due to the processual nature of the narratives, the European cultural heritage is constantly in the making and a European identity in a state of becoming.

Table 1: Strategies of narrating designated EHL sites (2007–2011) as European and the rhetorical means, the sources of narrative modes, and the notions of a European identity related to each strategy.

Strategies of narrating the EHL sites as European	Rhetorical means used in the narratives	Sources of narrative modes	Notions of a European identity
Strategy of European-wide interaction	• listing the European countries from where the artists, architects, or stylistic influences have arrived • emphasizing the sites' European-wide influence or distribution of the ideas or goods produced at the site • emphasizing the site as a meeting point for diverse people	EU rhetoric	consists of distinct but interactive national identities
Strategy of cultural grandeur	• emphasizing the outstanding quality, beauty, or splendor of the site • emphasizing the exemplary character of the site in relation to "European" architectural styles • referring to traditional forms of high culture	popular history	supra-national (high) cultural identity
Strategy of transnational ideas	• democracy, rights, and freedoms • coexistence of people, mutual respect, and equality between nations • humanitarian spirit, solidarity, and peace • entrepreneurship, mobility of workers, and free trade • Christianity	EU rhetoric	value identity
Strategy of anticipation of European integration	• emphasizing the site as historically anticipating the integration development of the EU • emphasizing the similarities between pre-national and post-national feelings of belonging • emphasizing the similarities between past and current mobility of people and migratory flows • emphasizing the site as a part of the history of the building of the EU	EU rhetoric	political EU identity
Strategy of self-evidence	• stating the site as European heritage and as reflecting a European identity • justifying the site's significance by its long history	popular history	*a priori* identity
Strategy of elevation of the nation	• emphasizing the particularity of the nation or nation-state and its achievements and significance among other nations in Europe • emphasizing the fostering of national cultures and identities as fostering of cultural diversity in Europe	national history	consists of distinct national identities

Note

1 This work was supported by the Academy of Finland (grant number SA21000012851, ID-ECC) and the University of Jyväskylä, Finland (mobility grant). The author conducted the research as a visiting fellow at the European University Institute, Florence, Italy.

References

Antonsich, Marco 2008: The Narration of Europe in 'National' and 'Post-national' Terms: Gauging the Gap between Normative Discourses and People's Views. *European Journal of Social Theory* 11:4, 505–522.

Archive of the Crown of Aragon. Application form for listing under the "European Heritage Label" scheme, 2007. Spanish Ministry of Culture, Spain. http://en.www.mcu.es/patrimonio/MC/PatrimonioEur/2007/ACA.html. Accessed April 12, 2013.

Ashworth, Gregory J. & Peter J. Larkham 1994: A Heritage for Europe: The Need, the Task, the Contribution. In: Gregory J. Ashworth & Peter J. Larkham (eds.), *Building a New Heritage: Tourism, Culture and Identity in the New Europe.* London: Routledge, pp. 1–9.

Ashworth, Gregory J. & Brian J. Graham 1997: Heritage, Identity and Europe. *Tijdschrift voor Economische en Sociale Geografie* 88:4, 381–388.

Ashworth, Gregory J., Brian J. Graham & John E. Tunbridge 2005: The Uses and Abuses of Heritage. In: G. Corsane (ed.), *Heritage, Museums and Galleries: An Introductory Reader.* London: Routledge, pp. 26–35.

Bacchilega, Christina 1997: *Postmodern Fairy Tales: Gender and Narrative Strategies.* Philadelphia: University of Pennsylvania Press.

Beck, Ulrich & Edgar Grande 2007: *Cosmopolitan Europe.* Cambridge: Polity.

Bee, Cristiano 2008: The 'Institutionally Constructed' European Identity: Citizenship and Public Sphere Narrated by the Commission. *Perspectives on European Politics and Society* 9:4, 431–450.

Bendix, Regina F., Aditya Eggert & Arnika Peselmann 2012: Introduction: Heritage Regimes and the State. In: Regina F. Bendix, Aditya Eggert & Arnika Peselmann (eds.), *Heritage Regimes and the State.* Göttingen Studies in Cultural Property 6. Göttingen: Universitätsverlag Göttingen, pp. 11–20.

Bortolotto, Chiara 2012: The French Inventory of Intangible Cultural Heritage: Domesticating a Global Paradigm into French Heritage Regime. In: Regina F. Bendix, Aditya Eggert & Arnika Peselmann (eds.), *Heritage Regimes and the State.* Göttingen Studies in Cultural Property 6. Göttingen: Universitätsverlag Göttingen, pp. 265–282.

Breakwell, Glynis M. 2004: Identity Change in the Context of the Growing Influence of European Union Institutions. In: Richard K. Herrmann, Thomas Risse & Marilynn B. Brewer (eds.), *Transnational Identities: Becoming European in the EU.* Oxford: Rowman & Battlefield, pp. 97–128.

van Bruggen, Martje 2006: *Symbols of the European Union: Flag and Anthem.* Groningen: University of Groningen.

Bruter, Michael 2003: Winning Hearts and Minds for Europe: The Impact of News and Symbols on Civic and Cultural European Identity. *Comparative Political Studies* 36:10, 1148–1179.

Bruter, Michael 2005: *Citizens of Europe? The Emergence of a Mass European Identity.* New York: Palgrave MacMillian.

Cathedral of St. Wenceslas and St. Stanislaus on Wawel Hill in Cracow. Application form for listing under the "European Heritage Label" scheme, 2007. Administration of the Wawel Cathedral, Poland. http://en.www.mcu.es/patrimonio/MC/PatrimonioEur/Red/Polonia_CatedraldeCracow.html. Accessed April 12, 2013.

Checkel, Jeffrey T. & Peter J. Katzenstein 2009: The Politicization of European Identities. In: Jeffrey T. Checkel & Peter J. Katzenstein (eds.), *European Identity.* Cambridge: Cambridge University Press, pp. 1–28.

Cunningham, Michael 1999: Saying Sorry: The Politics of the Apology. *The Political Quarterly* 70:3, 285–293.

Czarniawska, Barbara 2004: *Narratives in Social Science Research.* London: Sage.

Declaration on the initiative for a European Heritage Label. 25 January 2007. Madrid: Ministry of Education, Culture and Sport. http://en.www.mcu.es/patrimonio/MC/PatrimonioEur/docs/en declaracionMinistrosPatEu.pdf. Accessed April 12, 2013.

Delanty, Gerard 2002: Models of European Identity: Reconciling Universalism and Particularism. *Perspectives on European Politics and Society* 3:3, 345–359.

Delanty, Gerard 2009: The European Heritage: History, Memory, and Time. In: Chris Rumford (ed.), *The Sage Handbook of European Studies.* London: Sage, pp. 36–51.

Delanty, Gerard & Paul R. Jones 2002: European Identity and Architecture. *European Journal of Social Theory* 5:4, 453–466.

Delanty, Gerard & Chris Rumford 2005: *Rethinking Europe: Social Theory and the Implications of Europeanization.* London: Routledge.

Di Cesari, Chiara 2010: World Heritage and Mosaic Universalism: A View from Palestine. *Journal of Social Archaeology* 10:3, 299–324.

DuPlessis, Rachel Blau 1985: *Writing Beyond the Ending: Narrative Strategies of Twentieth-Century Women Writers.* Bloomington: Indiana University Press.

EC 2010: Impact Assessment: Commission Staff Working Document SEC(2010) 197, March 9, 2010. Brussels: European Commission.

EHL 2013a: Raeren stoneware (German-speaking community). Madrid: Ministry of Education, Culture and Sport. http://en.www.mcu.es/patrimonio/MC/PatrimonioEur/Red/Belgica_LosGresdeRaeren.html. Accessed April 12, 2013.

EHL 2013b: Hospice of St. Gothard. Madrid: Ministry of Education, Culture and Sport. http://en.www.mcu.es/patrimonio/MC/PatrimonioEur/Red/Suiza_Hospicio_San-Gotardo.html. Accessed April 12, 2013.

EHL 2013c: Cluny Abbey. Madrid: Ministry of Education, Culture and Sport. http://en.www.mcu.es/patrimonio/MC/PatrimonioEur/Red/Francia_AbadiaCluny.html. Accessed April 12, 2013.

EHL 2013d: Rundale Palace. Madrid: Ministry of Education, Culture and Sport. http://en.www.mcu.es/patrimonio/MC/PatrimonioEur/Red/Letonia_PalacioRundale.html. Accessed April 12, 2013.

EHL 2013e: Bradlo Mausoleum and the birthplace of General Milan Rastislav Štefánik. Madrid: Ministry of Education, Culture and Sport. http://en.www.mcu.es/patrimonio/MC/PatrimonioEur/Red/Eslovaquia_ArquitecturaReligiosa.html. Accessed April 12, 2013.

EHL 2013f: Industrial city of Tomas Bat'a in Zlin. Madrid: Ministry of Education, Culture and Sport. http://en.www.mcu.es/patrimonio/MC/PatrimonioEur/Red/RCheca_Ciudad_Tomas_Bata.html. Accessed April 12, 2013.

EHL 2013g: Pre-roman Religious Architecture: Saint Margaret's Church in Kopcany and Saint George's Church in Kostol'any pod Tribecom. Madrid: Ministry of Education, Culture and Sport. http://en.www.mcu.es/patrimonio/MC/PatrimonioEur/Red/Eslovaquia_ArquitecturaReligiosa.html. Accessed April 12, 2013.

EHL 2013h: Robert Schuman's House. Madrid: Ministry of Education, Culture and Sport. http://en.www.mcu.es/patrimonio/MC/PatrimonioEur/Red/Francia_Casa_RobertSchumann.html. Accessed April 12, 2013.

EHL 2013i: Historical Centre of Riga. Madrid: Ministry of Education, Culture and Sport. http://en.www.mcu.es/patrimonio/MC/PatrimonioEur/Red/Letonia_CentroRiga.html. Accessed April 12, 2013.

EHL 2013j: Milkalojus Konstantinas Ciurlionis. Madrid: Ministry of Education, Culture and Sport. http://en.www.mcu.es/patrimonio/MC/PatrimonioEur/Red/Lituania_ObrasMikalojusKonstantinas.html. Accessed April 12, 2013.

EHL 2013k: Krakow Cathedral. Madrid: Ministry of Education, Culture and Sport. http://en.www.mcu.es/patrimonio/MC/PatrimonioEur/Red/Polonia_CatedraldeCracow.html. Accessed April 12, 2013.

Eurobarometer Survey on Cultural Values within Europe 2007. Luxembourg: European Communities.

Herrmann, Richard K. & Marilynn B. Brewer 2004: Identities and Institutions: Becoming European in the EU. In: Richard K. Herrmann, Thomas Risse & Marilynn B. Brewer (eds.) *Transnational Identities: Becoming European in the EU*. Oxford: Rowman & Battlefield, pp. 1–24.

Hobsbawm, Eric 1983: Introduction: Inventing Tradition. In: Eric Hobsbawm & Terence Ranger (eds.), *The Invention of Tradition*. Cambridge: Cambridge University Press, pp. 1–14.

Ipsos 2007: *Enquête sur les Européens, les patrimoines de l'Europe et le patrimoine européen*. Paris: Ipsos/Ministère de la Culture et de la Communication.

Johler, Reinhard 2002: Local Europe: The Production of Cultural Heritage and the Europeanisation of Places. *Ethnologia Europaea* 32:2, 7–18.

Jones, Shannon & Jelena Subotic 2011: Fantasies of Power: Performing Europeanization on the European Periphery. *European Journal of Cultural Studies* 14:5, 542–557.

Kirshenblatt-Gimblett, Barbara 2006: World Heritage and Cultural Economics. In: Ivan Karp, Corinne A. Kratz, Lynn Szwaja & Thomas Ybarra-Frausto (eds.), *Museum Frictions: Public Culture/Global Transformation*. Durham & London: Duke University Press, pp. 161–202.

Kohli, Martin 2000: The Battlegrounds of European Identity. *European Societies* 2:2, 113–137.

Kourion. Application form for listing under the "European Heritage Label" scheme, 2007. Department of Antiquities, Cyprus. http://en.www.mcu.es/patrimonio/MC/PatrimonioEur/2007/ACA.html. Accessed April 12, 2013.

Lähdesmäki, Tuuli 2012: Rhetoric of Unity and Cultural Diversity in the Making of European Cultural Identity. *International Journal of Cultural Policy* 18:1, 59–75.

Lawler, Steph 2002: Narrative in Social Research. In: Tim May (ed.), *Qualitative Research in Action*. London: Sage, pp. 242–258.

MacCoshan, Andrew, David Gluck, Jenny Betts, Joe Clark, Simon Lee & Nathalie Pasquier 2009: *Support Services to Assist in the Preparation of the Impact Assessment and Ex-ante Evaluation of the European Heritage Label: Final Report*. Birmingham: ECOTEC.

Mälksoo, Maria 2009: The Memory Politics of Becoming European: The East European Subalterns and the Collective Memory of Europe. *European Journal of International Relations* 15:4, 653–680.

Mckeown, Max 2012: *The Strategy Book*. Harlow: Maverick & Strong.

Mitchell, Timothy 2001: Making the Nation: The Politics of Heritage in Egypt. In: Nezar AlSayyad (ed.), *Consuming Tradition, Manufacturing Heritage: Global Norms and Urban Form in the Age of Tourism*. London: Routledge, pp. 212–239.

Monastery of San Jeronimo de Yuste. Application form for listing under the "European Heritage Label" scheme, 2007. Yuste Academy and to the Jeronimo Religious Order, Spain. http://en.www.mcu.es/patrimonio/MC/PatrimonioEur/2007/Yuste.html. Accessed April 12, 2013.

Näss, Hans Erik 2010: The Ambiguities of Intercultural Dialogue: Critical Perspectives on the European Union's New Agenda for Culture. *Journal of Intercultural Communication* 23. http://www.immi.se/intercultural/. Accessed April 12, 2013.

Nic Craith, Máiréad 2012: Europe's (Un)common Heritage(s). *Traditiones* 41:2, 11–28.

Nora, Pierre 1996: From *Lieux de mémoire* to *Realms of Memory*. In: Pierre Nora (ed.), *Realms of Memory: Rethinking the French Past. Volume I: Conflicts and Divisions*. New York: Columbia University Press, pp. xv–xxiv.

Onken, Eva-Clarita 2007: The Baltic States and Moscow's 9 May Commemoration: Analysing Memory Politics in Europe. *Europe-Asia Studies* 59:1, 23–46.

Paasi, Anssi 2009: Regions and Regional Dynamics. In: Chris Rumford (ed.), *The Sage Handbook of European Studies*. London: Sage, pp. 464–485.

Peckham, Robert Shannan 2003: The Politics of Heritage and Public Culture. In: Robert Shannan Peckham (ed.), *Rethinking Heritage: Cultures and Politics in Europe*. London: I.B.Tauris, pp. 1–13.

Pichler, Florian 2008: European Identities from Below: Meanings of Identification with Europe. *Perspectives on European Politics and Society* 9:4, 411–430.

Pichler, Florian 2009: Cosmopolitan Europe: Views and Identity. *European Societies* 11:1, 3–24.

Ricoeur, Paul 1991: Narrative Identity. *Philosophy Today* 35:1, 73–81.

Risse, Thomas 2003: European Identity and the Heritage of National Culture. In: Robert Shannan Peckham (ed.), *Rethinking Heritage: Cultures and Politics in Europe*. London: I.B.Tauris, pp. 74–89.

Risse, Thomas 2006: Neofunctionalism, European Identity, and the Puzzles of European Integration. *Journal of European Public Policy* 12:2, 291–309.

Risse, Thomas 2010: *A Community of Europeans? Transnational Identities and Public Spheres*. New York: Cornell University Press.

Sassatelli, Monica 2006: The Logic of Europeanizing Cultural Policy. In: Ulrike H. Meinhof & Anna Triandafyllidou (eds.), *Transcultural Europe: Cultural Policy in a Changing Europe*. Basingstoke: Palgrave MacMillian, pp. 24–42.

Sassatelli, Monica 2009: *Becoming Europeans: Cultural Identity and Cultural Policies*. New York: Palgrave Macmillan.

Shore, Cris 1993: Inventing the 'People's Europe': Critical Approaches to European Community "Cultural Policy". *Man* 28:4, 779–800.

Shore, Cris 2000: *Building Europe: The Cultural Politics of European Integration*. London: Routledge.

Sites of the Reformation network. Application form for listing under the "European Heritage Label" scheme, 2010. Stiftung Luthergedenkstätten, Germany. http://en.www.mcu.es/patrimonio/MC/PatrimonioEur/Red/Alemania_Reforma.html. Accessed April 12, 2013.

Starzmann, Maria T. 2008: Cultural Imperialism and Heritage Politics in the Event of Armed Conflict: Prospects for an 'Activist Archaeology'. *Archaeologies* 4:3, 368–389.

Stråth, Bo 2002: A European Identity: To the Historical Limits of a Concept. *European Journal of Social Theory* 5:4, 387–401.

Szigetvár Castle. Application form for listing under the "European Heritage Label" scheme, 2009. Hungarian Treasury Property Directorate and Zrínyi Miklós Museum, Hungary. http://en.www.mcu.es/patrimonio/MC/PatrimonioEur/Red/Hungria_FortalezaSzigetvar.html Accessed 12 April, 2013.

The European Heritage Label, Rules of Procedure, Annex II, 25 January 2007. http://www.arhiv.mk.gov.si/fileadmin/mk.gov.si/pageuploads/min_eng/news/EHL/EHL_Criteria_for_Selection.pdf. Accessed April 12, 2013.

The historic and architectural ensemble of Rousse City Centre. Application form for listing under the "European Heritage Label" scheme, 2007. Municipality of Rousse, Bulgaria. http://en.www.mcu.es/patrimonio/MC/PatrimonioEur/Red/Bulgaria_Rousse.html. Accessed April 12, 2013.

The Reformed College and the Great Church in Debrecen. Application form for listing under the "European Heritage Label" scheme, 2007. The Hungarian Reformed Church, Hungary. http://en.www.mcu.es/patrimonio/MC/PatrimonioEur/Red/Hungria_IglesiaColegioDebrecen.html. Accessed April 12, 2013.

Treaty of Lisbon. Consolidated versions of the Treaty on European Union and the Treaty on the Functioning of the European Union, Council of the European Union, Brussels, April 30, 2008, 6655/1/08 REV 1.

"Vassil Levski" Memorial Complex. Application form for listing under the "European Heritage Label" scheme, 2007. Ministry of Culture, the National Museum "Vassil Levski", and the Municipality of Karlovo, Bulgaria. http://en.www.mcu.es/patrimonio/MC/PatrimonioEur/Red/Bulgaria_MemorialVassil_Levski.html. Accessed April 12, 2013.

Vázquez, David J. 2011: *Triangulations: Narrative Strategies for Navigating Latino Identity*. Minneapolis: University of Minnesota Press.

Tuuli Lähdesmäki, Ph.D., is a senior researcher at the Department of Art and Culture Studies, University of Jyväskylä, Finland. Her major research interests include identity and heritage politics, urban space, and discursive meaning-making processes in contemporary culture. Her latest research project, funded by the Academy of Finland, was titled Identity Politics in Pécs, Tallinn, and Turku as European Capitals of Culture (ID-ECC).
(tuuli.lahdesmaki@jyu.fi)

The Power of Song

Nonviolent National Culture in the Baltic Singing Revolution

Guntis Šmidchens

456 pp · hb
ISBN 978 87 635 4148 0
DKK 290 · $ 50 · € 39

The Power of Song shows how the people of Estonia, Latvia, and Lithuania confronted a military superpower and achieved independence in the Baltic "Singing Revolution". When attacked by Soviet soldiers in public displays of violent force, singing Balts maintained faith in nonviolent political action.

As an inspiration to all nations, the nonviolent Baltic independence movement revolutionized each country through singing and smiling. The "Singing Revolution" is indeed the essence of the Baltic way, and began in 1987 as a public revolt against Soviet restrictions on free speech and assembly. The revolutions and following elections in 1990 resulted in three separate governments and a declaration of independence from the Soviet Union.

The Power of Song seeks to answer questions such as why the struggle for Baltic independence came to be called the Singing Revolution? What did they sing? And what role did singing play in the Estonian, Latvian, and Lithuanian campaigns of political mobilization and nonviolent action? Furthermore, and uniquely for this publication, it explores, in great depth, the songs that gave the revolution its name, translating and interpreting more than 110 choral, rock, and folk songs in their poetic, cultural, and historical context.

Guntis Šmidchens *is the Kazickas Family Endowed Professor in Baltic Studies in the Scandinavian Studies Department at the University of Washington.*

MUSEUM TUSCULANUM PRESS
UNIVERSITY OF COPENHAGEN

Birketinget 6 · DK–2300 Copenhagen S

TEL   +45 3234 1414   WEB   www.mtp.dk
FAX   +45 3258 1488   ORDERS   order@mtp.dk

Danish Folktales, Legends, & Other Stories

Timothy R. Tangherlini

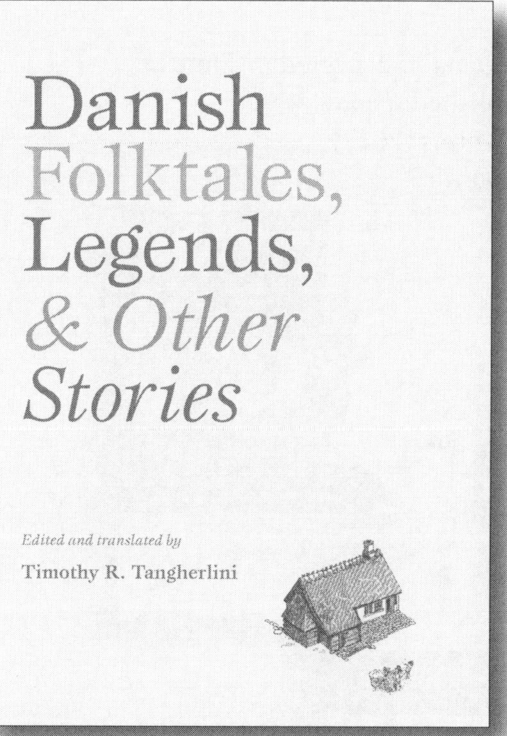

Danish Folktales, Legends, & Other Stories is a collection of translated and annotated Nordic folklore that presents the full repertoires of five storytellers along with extensive archival material. The printed book presents some of the most compelling stories of these important storytellers, accompanied by historical and biographical introductions. Of a length suitable for course use, the book provides a substantive and enjoyable encounter with Danish folklore.

The Danish Folklore Nexus, on the accompanying DVD, includes the storytellers' full repertoires, plus five hundred additional stories in both Danish and English, along with essays on the changing political, social, and economic landscapes of nineteenth-century Denmark; the history of folklore scholarship; critical approaches to folklore; and comprehensive biographies of the storytellers. It also provides links between related stories and interactive maps that will allow readers to see where the stories are set and where they were collected, as well as a mechanism to search for themes and topics across all the stories.

256 pp · hb · incl. DVD
ISBN 978 87 635 4118 3
DKK 280 · $ 48 · € 38

Timothy R. Tangherlini *is Professor of folklore and chair of the Scandinavian Section at the University of California, Los Angeles.*

MUSEUM TUSCULANUM PRESS
UNIVERSITY OF COPENHAGEN

Birketinget 6 · DK–2300 Copenhagen S
TEL +45 3234 1414   WEB www.mtp.dk
FAX +45 3258 1488   ORDERS order@mtp.dk

Ethnologia Europaea
JOURNAL OF EUROPEAN ETHNOLOGY

Ethnologia Europaea is a lively and interdisciplinary, peer-reviewed journal with a focus on European cultures and societies. It carries material of great interest not only for European ethnologists and anthropologists but also for sociologists, social historians and scholars involved in cultural studies.

An impression of the areas covered by the journal is reflected in some of the thematic topics of the issues recently published: *Foodways Redux* (2013), *Imagined Families in Mobile Worlds* (2012), *Irregular Ethnographies* (2011), *Performing Nordic Spaces* (2010), *Sense of Community* (2009), *Europe* (2008), *Double Homes, Double Lives?* (2007).

For more information on purchase and subscription visit
www.mtp.dk/ethnologia_europaea

Museum Tusculanum Press : : University of Copenhagen
Birketinget 6, 2300 Copenhagen S, Denmark
WWW.MTP.DK

INSTRUCTIONS TO AUTHORS

Ethnologia Europaea is an interdisciplinary peer-reviewed journal with a focus on European cultures and societies. The journal was first published in 1967 and since then it has acquired a central position in the international and interdisciplinary co-operation between scholars inside and outside Europe. Two issues are published yearly in a printed version and a digital one.

The journal welcomes high quality papers from European ethnology but also from social/cultural and historical anthropological perspectives as well as from scholarly fields such as human geography, sociology, cultural history, and cultural studies.

To find out if your contribution fits in, you may start by e-mailing the two editors a short abstract or outline. To familiarize yourself with our profile, take a look at some recent issues. An impression of the areas covered by the journal is reflected in some of the thematic topics of recent special issues: *Imagined Families in Mobile Worlds* (2012), *Irregular Ethnographies* (2011), *Performing Nordic Spaces* (2010), *Sense of Community* (2009). Please visit the publisher's website: www.mtp.dk/ethnologia_europaea.

Authors of successfully published articles receive one copy of the journal and the article in a pdf-file.

Submission and format: Manuscripts (in English) should be sent to the two editors as a computer file via e-mail. Authors will be notified after the peer-review process about acceptance, rejection, or desired alterations.

Papers should not exceed 12,000 words. Too many grades of headings should be avoided. Long quotations should be marked by indentations and double line spacing.

British or American English may be used, but adhering to one or the other consistently is essential. For non-native English speakers it is a precondition for publishing that final accepted manuscripts are checked by a professional copy-editor or translator.

Abstract, keywords and author presentation: Five keywords as well as an abstract should accompany the manuscript. The abstract should be at the most 125 words, outline the main arguments, the empirical basis and stress the conclusions. A short presentation (approximately three sentences) of the author should be included, describing title, position, research interests and for example a recent publication. Please check and copy the style of a recent issue of *Ethnologia Europaea*.

Illustrations: You may supply suggested illustrations for the editors to choose from. For the final version the chosen illustrations with accompanying captions (including photographer or source) should be provided with the highest possible resolution. Desired positions of illustrations should be marked in the text. The author needs to secure publishing rights for all illustrations. The journal does not pay for illustration costs and authors will be asked for a written statement about permissions.

Endnotes and references: Endnotes should be used sparingly. If acknowledgements appear they should be placed in the first endnote. Please check that all references are included in the bibliography and vice versa. Bibliographic references in the text are given as (Hobsbawm & Ranger 1983; Shaw 1995, 2000). In the bibliography the following system is used:

Bauman, Zygmunt 1990: Modernity and Ambivalence. In: Mike Featherstone (ed.), *Global Culture: Nationalism, Globalization and Modernity.* London: Sage Publications, pp. 143–169.

Czarniawska, Barbara & Orvar Löfgren (eds.) 2012: *Managing Overflow in Affluent Societies.* London: Routledge.

Timm, Elisabeth 2012: Grounding the Family: Locality and Its Discontents in Popular Genealogy. *Ethnologia Europaea* 42:2, 36–50. www.mtp.hum.ku.dk/details.asp?eln=300309. Accessed June 5, 2013.

Disorder and order are among the principles through which
the articles in this issue are connected. Peter Jan Margry grasps
the exuberant excesses surrounding the Dutch monarch's
birthday with the term "mobocracy" and sees in the suspension
of rules a means to reconcile Dutch republicanism with the
anachronism of a monarchical system. Ongoing disorder of a
rather different nature is experienced by migrant workers from
Poland in Denmark. Niels Jul Nielsen and Marie Sandberg
accompany them at work and in their different home settings
and analyse the divergent interplay of the Polish labour niche
and family dynamics on different constructions of "orderly work
conditions". Stefan Groth uncovers the structuring power of
new tools and events to measure performance in recreational
cycling; competitive norms are shown to permeate a leisure
activity. Old age, too, is not free from the structuring arm of
social and health regimes. Through his analysis of billiards – a
game favoured by the older men he studies – Aske Juul Lassen
critiques aging policies striving to "activate" the elderly and
overlooking the rhythms inherent to a traditional game – and
activity. The issue concludes with Tuuli Lähdesmäki's comparison
of how local heritage actors choose to narrate the transnationally
launched European Heritage Label. Within an initiative to foster
Europeanization, she finds actors formulating European identities
in different moulds.